# PRAYING THROUGH OUR LIFETRAPS

## A Psycho-Spiritual Path to Freedom

John Cecero, S.J., Ph.D.

**Resurrection Press**
An Imprint of
**CATHOLIC BOOK PUBLISHING CO.**
Totowa • New Jersey

First published in September 2002 by
Catholic Book Publishing/Resurrection Press
77 West End Road
Totowa, NJ 07512

ISBN 1-878718-70-3
Library of Congress Catalog Card Number: 2002107688

Cover design and background photo by John Murello

Printed in the United States of America

# Contents

# Foreword

THIS book is an extremely rich, clear, and practical guide to integrating the basic theory and therapeutic approach of Schema Therapy (ST) with the spiritual wisdom accumulated through the centuries in the Christian tradition. In *Praying Through Our Lifetraps: A Psycho-Spiritual Path to Freedom*, John Cecero skillfully describes many of the key "lifetraps" faced by all of us, including people engaged in psychotherapy, spiritual direction, and pastoral counseling. He articulates intervention strategies that are informed both by ST and by his own knowledge of spirituality—that will serve as an invaluable resource for mental health and interpersonal satisfaction.

Over the past decade, in the course of articulating and continually revising the principles and techniques of Schema Therapy, I have noticed that for some patients with certain kinds of life issues, the standard cognitive, behavioral, experiential, and therapy relationship interventions that comprise ST are not enough. For example, for some people who are struggling with the abandonment lifetrap in the context of permanent loss, either through divorce or death, it is difficult to successfully challenge the notion that people will ultimately leave. It appears to me that many of the spiritual strategies identified in this book are very useful as an adjunctive component of ST. Indeed, a schema therapist might confront the abandonment lifetrap with the assurance of an ever-present, divine love that will never leave the patient.

As a clinical psychologist and seasoned ST practitioner, John Cecero is well acquainted with the broad diversity of clinical issues presented in this book. His clinical formulations of the issues he presents are both theoretically sound and entirely consistent with the ST approach. At the same time, his religious background and pastoral training for the Jesuit priesthood clearly inform and support the soundness of his recommendations about ways of integrating these formulations and recommendations for spiritually-oriented patients.

This book coherently brings together a body of research findings and clinical techniques that span the disciplines of developmental and clinical psychology, along with the speculative and applied domains of theology and spirituality. Throughout the book, Dr. Cecero focuses on the assessment and treatment contributions of these findings, and he carefully explores their implications for alleviating the personal distress and interpersonal disruptions that are so often the effects of lifetraps.

The final section of the book is dedicated specifically to the application of the author's "psycho-spiritual" approach to various therapeutic modalities (e.g., professional counseling, spiritual direction, and spiritual reading). He demonstrates how the mental health and interpersonal benefits of integrating ST and spirituality can be sustained through a variety of contexts, and shows the reader how to benefit from these strategies, both within and outside the context of psychotherapy.

In sum, this book represents an exciting and welcome addition to the ST repertoire of treatment interventions. It will no doubt assist countless people who will see themselves and their lifetraps in these pages, and will want to draw on both psychological insight and spiritual wisdom to lead happier and more fulfilling lives.

*Jeffrey E. Young, Ph.D.*

# Preface

ON September 11, 2001, just as I was beginning to write this book, at a little less than a mile away from my desk, the World Trade Center attacks interrupted the course of our history and generated unprecedented levels of fear and anxiety right here on our doorstep. In the aftermath, many individuals and groups have shared with me in clinical and community encounters their own emotional reactions to this horrific event. For those with pre-existing trauma in their lives—including experiences of childhood abuse or neglect, or more recent experiences of the death of a loved one, a divorce, or some other destabilizing life event—this terrorist assault was even more difficult to accept. It highlighted a sense of prevailing danger and vulnerability to harm in daily living. For others with anxiety and depressive disorders, this event exacerbated their symptoms and made it all the more difficult to find peace in their lives. And for those with substance use disorders, cravings and relapse became more prevalent, as many looked for the familiar—if toxic—sources of comfort and detachment in these troublesome times. For those fortunate enough to be unscathed by such distress prior to that horrendous day, their innocence was shattered, and their world suddenly became a dangerous and unpredictable place.

Against this backdrop of fears, doubts, and anxieties, the completion of the present text took on even more significance for me. While the lifetraps described in this book are mostly developed in response to individual problematic experiences with parents, siblings, spouses and peers, they are made even more pervasive when responding to collective events such as those of September 11, which have created an atmosphere of fear and uncertainty, fertile ground for the enhancement of lifetrap beliefs.

My clinical experience in applying Jeffrey Young's Schema Therapy to treat patients who are struggling with a variety of fears and anxieties—including concerns about being abandoned or rejected, or unsuccessful attempts to take care of themselves on their own, or with difficulties in recognizing their own needs and wishes—has underscored the value of this therapeutic approach. Through changing problematic ways of thinking about themselves, initiating new behaviors to put the more positive thoughts into practice, permitting the expression of the negative feelings that are often ignored or avoided, and by creating a therapy relationship that fosters the development and practice of a new way of relating interpersonally, Schema Therapy represents a significant advance to existing modes of psychotherapy.

At the same time, I have become increasingly aware of the rich tradition of prayer and spiritual practice that can supplement this therapeutic approach for people of faith. In the course of therapy, when someone is struggling to believe that anyone cares for them or recognizes their needs, my being able to point out that there is a God whose love is everlasting and ever available to us, and that access to God will foster faith and courage have been invaluable tools in confronting fear-based lifetraps.

In many conferences and workshops for clergy and laity alike, I have articulated some of the ways that integrating spirituality into clinical practice can better address key fears in life. It seems to me that lifetrap theory and practice is particularly suited for this kind of integration, as the perspective of lifetraps is fear and the goal of spirituality is freedom.

This book has afforded me the opportunity to systematically address this integration in what I call a psycho-spiritual approach. It will not be appropriate for all people seeking recovery from lifetraps, but for those who are open to a religious or spiritual influence in their lives, I believe that it will open additional avenues for healing and growth. I hope that reading this text will assist you in your search for truth and wholeness.

# Part I

# Lifetraps and the Power of Prayer

WHEN life becomes difficult to bear, as you go through periods of trial and distress that are often triggered by unexpected
changes in your personal or professional life, it is important to
locate sources of help, encouragement, and hope to assist you.
For some, a visit to a psychologist or other mental health worker is on the short list of steps to take for guidance and possibly
some form of treatment. For others, particularly for those with
a spiritual orientation and affiliation with a religious tradition,
the priest or minister is the one to whom you may more likely
turn for direction and support.

While the mental health worker is more likely to offer
strategies for responding more adaptively to deal with the
problems at hand by using standard psychological techniques
in a therapeutic framework, the pastoral minister is more likely to refer to your life of faith and personal relationship with
God, using your prayer life and spiritual strategies to support
and sustain your hope and confidence during the difficult
period.

For the person of faith, whether you go to a therapist or a
priest, there is more than likely something missing from the
feedback that you are receiving. Because there has been little
communication between mental health and pastoral ministers
about the kinds of support that are profitably offered to those
seeking their assistance, there have been few systematic
attempts to integrate psychological strategies with spiritual
approaches to health and peace of mind.

This book is intended to present a way for you to use both
psychological and spiritual resources in dealing with life's
problems. Named a *psycho-spiritual* approach, this strategy

relies both on the clinical wisdom of a particular school of pyschotherapy, Schema Therapy (ST), and on a tradition of prayer and spiritual practices that can be used in conjunction with the therapeutic techniques of ST.

Following a description in Chapter 1 of the kinds of life problems, or *lifetraps*, that have been identified by the authors of ST and that are commonly associated with significant distress in personal and interpersonal situations, Chapter 2 describes the kinds of prayer movements that Christians have used for centuries to approach the living God and find peace and strength.

# 1

## Lifetraps—from the Beginning

### How Did You Ever Become Who You Are Today?

HAVE you ever found yourself walking down a busy street or simply stopping to rest somewhere and looking out at the range of people passing by, some laughing, others engaged in serious conversation, some well-groomed, others barely clothed, some heading home, others homeless? And have you ever wondered what is driving each of these people to behave as they are, and what events or circumstances in life may account for where they are today? Then, perhaps you turn your attention to your own life, and you wonder how you ended up in the career, marriage or other significant relationships that have become so much a part of your life. Are you happy with your choices? Are they the right ones still?

For me, perhaps the most compelling motivation to pursue a vocation to the priesthood and a career as a clinical psychologist has been my enduring interest in figuring out what influences the choices that people make through the ordinary and exceptional events of life.

Each of us has a unique story to account for our decisions and present life circumstances. For most of us, our recollection of the story begins with memories of childhood, parents and siblings, and significant friends along the way. But our stories truly begin, of course, before we can even remember or put into words the context and quality of these interactions in our lives.

Being male or female starts us off in different directions with a unique set of interests and interactions with the world. Whether we were little or big, chubby or petite probably made a difference in how our parents responded to us, particularly around issues of feeding. Our temperament also contributes to our personal story in a significant way. Some of us are shy by nature, wary of interpersonal interactions, and others learned to treat us accordingly, sometimes by ignoring us. Others are more socially adept, gregarious, playful, and the world responds in kind, with more physical affection and attention. Intelligence, too, plays a key role in our developing selves. Our level of curiosity, language skills, and capacity to engage others in responding to our questions all largely determine the quality of our childhood experience.

As our gender, temperament, and intelligence are biologically determined, they are indelible and usually unchangeable aspects of our story that we must simply accept as the givens of our lives. There are, however, other parts to our story that are environmentally driven—influenced by our parents, siblings, and peers—and these aspects of our life experience, although just as influential as those biological factors, are indeed more amenable to change.

Consider, for example, the influence of those earliest teachers in your lives, your parents. Do you recall a loving, affectionate father who was empathic, caring, and available for soothing when you were hurt or disappointed, or do you instead recall a more emotionally distant, dispassionate father who was unavailable for guidance, support, and protection? When you think of your mother, do you recollect images of a woman who supported your independence and curiosity, or one who taught you to fear the world and to cling to her and her wishes for you? Similarly, when you remember your brothers and sisters, do you recall support, love, and healthy competition, or instead are your memories more tinted with jealousy, rejection, and unrelentingly hurtful comparisons? These early childhood family experiences with parents and siblings play a significant role in subsequent life directions.

Early environmental influences on our lives are not restricted, of course, to our parents and siblings. Teachers, mentors, counselors, and extended family and friends can function as invaluable resources to assist us in coping with the painful emotions resulting from troublesome interactions with parents and siblings. In many cases, their influence may have contributed to a healthier life direction than one that would have otherwise been chosen by an emotionally troubled or confused young person.

For example, if your parents set a standard of perfection for you, where nothing less than a perfect performance at school was acceptable, then when the inevitable below average grade entered your world, and you were feeling like an absolutely worthless person, a sensitive teacher or counselor in whom you had some degree of trust or confidence might have been able to help you. Their acceptance of your limitations might have supported a more resilient sense of self-esteem, even in the face of disappointment or failure. Conversely, if your parents were more neglectful or disinterested in your academic, creative, or athletic performance, an involved teacher or coach might have contributed significantly to your sense of self-worth and increased your interest in these activities. Psychological research has demonstrated again and again the powerful influence of teacher expectations on school performance. When students believe that their teacher has expectations for their success, they are more likely to live up to those standards, and sadly the converse is also true.

While parents are largely responsible for your values and beliefs, peer interactions are probably more responsible for the degree of your sense of interpersonal comfort—your sense of fitting in with others. Were you popular with your classmates and neighboring children, or were you ignored, or worse ridiculed and excluded from games? Depending upon your experiences with peers, you may find yourself even today reaching out to friends for play or comfort, or else avoiding others out of fear or disinterest.

In a very real sense, you have become who you are as a result of all of these factors, biological and environmental. They account for whether you feel secure in relationships with your spouse, partners, and friends, or if you are more cautious and suspicious about the enduring nature of these relationships. They likewise influence your sense of responsibility and freedom to make your own choices, and the degree to which you seek perfection in your life. As such, they continue to influence your inner sense of peace and tranquility, as well as your sense of satisfaction with, and commitment to, personal and professional relationships.

## Lifetraps—Getting in the Way of Your Peace and Fulfillment

While most of us may readily acknowledge that these childhood influences play some role in our present sense of peace and fulfillment today, it is not easy to sort through the diverse and sometimes conflicting psychological theories to determine the extent of their ongoing influence. Some theories emphasize the role of biology and temperament above everything, suggesting that parenting has been exaggerated as an influential part of our development. Other theories stress the unconscious, fantasized relationships with our parents as the key developmental influences. Still others advocate ignoring the childhood antecedents of our thinking and feeling in favor of a focus on the current environmental reinforcements of our behavior.

One encouraging new approach to the understanding of the influence of childhood experiences on current emotional and interpersonal functioning has been introduced and elaborated upon by Jeffrey Young, author of *Cognitive Therapy for Personality Disorders: A Schema-Focused Therapy Approach.* Young explains that problematic childhood experiences with parents, siblings and peers may lead to the development of *lifetraps* (alternatively labeled in his work as "early maladaptive schemas," which he defines as broad, pervasive themes that are comprised of memories, cognitions, emotions and bodily sensations that are developed during childhood or adolescence and are elaborated upon throughout one's lifetime, making them resistant to change and leading the lifetrapped person to experience significant emotional distress and marked difficulties with interpersonal functioning.

For example, if you grew up with one or both parents who were emotionally unstable or unpredictable in their emotional expression, where there were angry outbursts or unexpected reactions to your stated needs or wishes, then you are prone to develop an *abandonment* lifetrap. According to this lifetrap belief, you continue to suspect in your adult life that significant others (partners, friends, close colleagues) will be erratically present and ultimately unreliable, because like your parents, they too will abandon you emotionally, if not physically, through death or divorce. Imagine the degree of chronic anxiety associated with this lifetrap, as well as the pattern of failed relationships that are likely to result from it.

Or, if one or another of your parents was overprotective, fearful about your ability to survive and take care of yourself outside of his or her immediate protection, then you are likely to develop the *dependence* lifetrap. You might strongly suspect that you are incapable of handling life's ordinary responsibilities on your own and become overly reliant on others to assist you in even the most mundane tasks. You will likewise be very hesitant to take risks, believing that you will likely fail to summon the personal and professional resources to see a challenging new task through to completion.

## Which are Your Lifetraps?

In the beginning of their book on lifetraps, *Reinventing Your Life*, Jeffrey Young and Janet Klosko present a Lifetrap Questionnaire designed to assist the reader in coming up with a preliminary identification of his or her own lifetraps. Below is an adaptation of that questionnaire which includes only the lifetraps that will be described in more detail in this book.

Rate each of the next fourteen statements in terms of how true each is of you on this six-point scale.

### Scoring Key

1   Completely untrue of me
2   Mostly untrue of me
3   Slightly more true than untrue of me
4   Moderately true of me
5   Mostly true of me
6   Describes me perfectly

## The Lifetrap Quiz

_____ 1. I try very hard to hold on to people I'm close to and often end up driving them away.

_____ 2. I believe that I'm going to end up alone

_____ 3. I don't trust people easily.

_____ 4. I am afraid that people will emotionally hurt me.

_____ 5. I do not feel I can deal well with life's responsibilities on my own; I rely on others to help me.

_____ 6. My parents and I tend to be very involved in each other's lives and problems.

_____ 7. I have never had enough love and attention in my life.

_____ 8. People have not been there to guide me in life.

_____ 9. I worry that if I don't do what others ask of me that I'll be rejected.

_____10. I worry a lot about pleasing people.

_____11. I am a very competitive person.

_____12. I am preoccupied with performance and success above pleasure and relaxation.

_____13. I have a hard time making myself follow rules and regulations.

_____14. I can't take "no" for an answer.

## Scoring Instructions

Each of the seven lifetraps that will be examined in detail in this book is briefly assessed in this questionnaire. There will be more extensive questionnaires for each of them in the chapters that follow. For now, simply look at your responses to the above statements, and if you have rated any of them a 4, 5, or 6, then you may have the lifetrap associated with that statement.

Two statements correspond to each of the following lifetraps:

| Statements | Lifetrap |
|:---:|:---:|
| 1 and 2 | Abandonment |
| 3 and 4 | Mistrust and Abuse |
| 5 and 6 | Dependence |
| 7 and 8 | Emotional Deprivation |
| 9 and 10 | Subjugation |
| 11 and 12 | Unrelenting Standards |
| 13 and 14 | Entitlement |

Now that you have some preliminary idea of your own specific lifetraps, you may want to use that information to guide your reading of Part II of this book, where each of the lifetrap patterns is described in more detail, and a more thorough questionnaire for each of them is presented in each of those chapters.

On the surface, these lifetrap themes may seem irrational, even as you think about them and feel their emotional effects. After all, why would you automatically expect that a person whom you've been dating for the past couple of years would probably leave you because he found someone else more attractive? Why can't you allow yourself to believe that his assurances of love and commitment are real and enduring? Your rational mind and your experience with this person tell you that all the evidence supports the truthfulness of his claim, and yet a side of you—the lifetrapped side—continues to fuel fears and doubts about his fidelity. What makes these lifetraps so resistant to reason?

Young proposes that it is precisely because these lifetraps have their origin in frustrating, sometimes traumatic depriva- tions of core childhood needs. Moreover, different lifetraps cor- respond to different kinds of deprivation or trauma. In general, the lifetraps are organized around five core developmental needs, such that when any of these are not adequately met in childhood, certain corresponding lifetraps are likely to develop:

| Core Needs | Lifetraps |
|---|---|
| 1. Connection with a stable caretaker | Abandonment |
| | Emotional Deprivation |
| | Mistrust and Abuse |
| 2. Autonomy | Dependence |
| 3. Realistic Limits | Entitlement |
| 4. Self-Directedness | Subjugation |
| 5. Spontaneity and Play | Unrelenting Standards |

## Connection

The very first need that we all experience as children is for emotional connection to our primary caretaker. Developmental psychologists John Bowlby and Mary Ainsworth have demon- strated that primates are hard-wired for emotional connection, and that the establishment of a secure attachment is essential to the infant, even above physical sustenance. If you experienced a traumatic emotional disconnection early in life, perhaps through the death or divorce of your parents, or through the emotional instability of one or both parents, then you are pre- disposed to the *abandonment* lifetrap as described above.

As children, we all need to feel secure, safe, and stable, while receiving emotional nurturance in the form of empathy. Self-psychologists claim that our self-esteem, or the capacity to regulate our feelings of self-worth, even in the face of adversity and failure, is essentially linked to our receiving praise and admiration as children. For example, if you came home from school with a drawing to show your parents, and the response from them was disinterest, or worse criticism, then your development of a healthy sense of self-worth was seriously compromised. You would be vulnerable to developing the lifetrap of *emotional deprivation,* a chronic fear that people are unable or unwilling to understand you and are essentially incapable of providing the strength, guidance, or direction that you may need to be happy.

Suppose, for example, that you were physically, sexually, or emotionally abused or neglected as a child by one or both of your parents. In that case, you experienced perhaps the most extreme form of disconnection, and you are likely to develop a *mistrust/abuse* lifetrap, which is the fear that others will harm, abuse, cheat, or manipulate you intentionally. You will likely live your life in fear and suspicion of the motives and deeds of others.

## Autonomy

If you have ever observed toddlers at play, especially in the beginning of the second year of life, you will notice their fascination with sliding down their mothers' laps and disappearing for awhile around the corner, only to reappear to see if she is still there and looking for them. In addition to these games of hiding and finding, disappearing and reappearing, they are likewise enchanted with the word "no," and they use it frequently. Margaret Mahler and Selma Fraiberg, experts on early development, point out that the underlying issue here is the search for autonomy, the wish to say to that loving parent or to the primary caretaker, "I can do it on my own; I don't need you!" If your parent or primary caretaker was wise and tolerant enough to support these explorations away from her protective glance and not too threatened by your protestations, then you probably developed a healthy sense of autonomy, i.e., the secure notion that you can go out on your own, or disagree, and not be alienated or punished for it. If, on the other hand, your parent was too enmeshed with you, trying to live through you, and was not supportive of your wish to explore the world apart from her or him, then you are likely to have developed the lifetrap of *dependence* as described above.

## Realistic Limits

Perhaps one of the most counterintuitive facts of child-rearing for parents is the notion that setting limits is essential to the normal growth and development of their child. Parents are more often than not inclined to indulge their children, to gratify their wishes as much as possible, sometimes even beyond their realistic means. This permissiveness and overindulgence may lead to the lifetrap of *entitlement*, a belief that you are superior to other people, not one of the ordinary human beings around you, and therefore not bound by their rules and regulations. I once had a patient with this lifetrap who could not tolerate riding the subway with all of those "ordinary" people, and waiting for service or amenities was experienced as a humiliation. This lifetrap precludes the development of empathy for others, because you are so self-absorbed, and often accounts for a great deal of social isolation.

## Self-Directedness

As little children, all of us are schooled in emotions, while learning to acknowledge, label, and identify feelings, and to express them appropriately to others. This process requires that parents pay close attention to the emotions of children, even before they have the words to express them. Cries, shouts, flailing of arms—all of these expressions, ideally, ought to be met by parents with recognition and curiosity. Rather than dismiss or punish a child for calling attention to her wishes, parents are well-advised to help the child identify her feelings and find words or other expressions to communicate them. In the absence of this self-directedness, the child develops the notion that her own feelings are irrelevant or at best secondary to the feelings and demands of the parents. These kinds of experiences may result in the lifetrap of *subjugation,* an enduring belief that others' needs and desires are more important than yours, and an excessive focus on meeting their needs to avoid criticism or rejection. This lifetrap frequently breeds resentment and anger at those who make demands on your time—parents, partners, children, colleagues. It becomes difficult, if not impossible, to say no, either because you are so afraid of the imagined consequences or because you have lost touch with what you really want or feel after so many years of looking outside for direction, and not within. Eventually, however, the underlying rage fostered by this lifetrap does manage to surface, often in the form of uncontrolled temper outbursts, psychosomatic symptoms, or substance abuse problems.

## Spontaneity and Play

Selma Fraiberg stated that the work of childhood is play. The many and varied expressions of feelings, impulses, desires, and fears are symbolized in play. From astronaut to bus driver, roles are rehearsed and exchanged, and children use play to express their fantasies, to relax, and to initiate and sustain social contacts. Parents who encourage play and spontaneity contribute to the development of creative, well-balanced children. Some parents, however, are so rigid about performance and perfection that they underestimate the importance of play, emphasizing duty over pleasure at every turn. This parental attitude may foster the lifetrap of *unrelenting standards*—the belief that all of your time should be spent in achieving goals— and in doing so without fault or flaw. There is no time for play, and every activity is so serious that the fun is sapped even out of otherwise enjoyable work. Learning something new is not stimulating; it is instead another opportunity for mistakes and imperfection. Over time, your world becomes so pressured by these internalized standards of behavior and performance that you forget how to relax and refresh yourself. You are never very far from anxiety, depression, and hostility.

## What Keeps These Lifetraps Alive for You Now?

Once these lifetraps are established through the kinds of frustrating or traumatic childhood experiences just described, they continue to exert their influence on adult feeling, thinking, and behaving. Jeff Young has identified three processes by which we perpetuate the harmful influence of our lifetraps, and he refers to these processes as (1) maintenance, (2) avoidance, and (3) compensation.

Once you develop the lifetrap of emotional deprivation, for example, you maintain and even strengthen that belief by continuing to mistakenly expect that your needs for emotional support will never be met by anyone. You focus exclusively on any hints of unreliability in the other person, to the exclusion of those traits that may be redeeming, endearing, or promising for a real mutual relationship. Your behavior, too, will contribute to maintaining this lifetrap. For example, believing that people are not capable of satisfying your need for empathy and understanding, you may too easily settle down with partners who are less likely to be emotionally reliable, and each time they demonstrate their unreliability you will only become more convinced that your lifetrap is indeed accurate.

Lifetraps are likewise strengthened by a process of avoidance. Because the fears associated with these lifetraps are so difficult to face directly, you may think, feel, and behave in ways designed, consciously or unconsciously, to avoid facing the upsetting lifetrap belief. For example, if you have the lifetrap of subjugation, and you feel obliged to act in certain ways as a worker or spouse in order to avoid anger or retaliation, then you may be prone to overlook or minimize the toll that those demands are taking on your life (e.g., "It's not that much to ask" or "I ought to be less selfish about my time"). You may also block the feelings, frequently anger and resentment, that often accompany the subjugation lifetrap. Sometimes people turn to alcohol, drugs, overeating, sexual promiscuity, and other avoidant behaviors to numb the pain. You will likely avoid situations that may trigger the subjugation lifetrap. For example, if you foresee new demands at home or at work, you may try to avoid them, believing that it is impossible to be responsible and also to take care of yourself at the same time. You believe that responsibilities require self-annihilation.

Sometimes people confront their lifetrap fears head on and attempt to compensate for them by doing exactly the opposite of what the lifetrap dictates for them. For example, if you have a dependence lifetrap, and you believe that you are not capable of handling the ordinary responsibilities of life without extra-ordinary help from others, you may compensate for this belief by taking on some new project or making some new decision without the consultation or help of anyone else. While this may sound like an effective way of overcoming the lifetrap, the problem with this strategy is that it frequently goes too far; the person ends up taking on too much responsibility and making decisions or choices that really would have required the assis-tance of others for successful outcomes. When you experience failure or disappointment in this circumstance, then you are likely to believe the lifetrap now more than ever.

## Overcoming Lifetraps—A Psycho-Spiritual Approach

Rooted in childhood fears and anxieties, lifetraps involve unhealthy patterns of thinking, feeling, behaving, and relating to others, and each of these aspects of human living must be addressed in order to change them. For some people, the life-traps are so rigid and maladaptive that they cause considerable emotional pain and interpersonal problems. Psychotherapy may well be indicated for such individuals. For others, the life-traps are clearly operative, but their effects on emotional well-being and interpersonal functioning may be less toxic. For such people, there may be other non-clinical settings where lifetraps may be addressed and changed. For people of faith, spiritual direction or pastoral counseling may serve as such a setting. Whether through psychotherapy or not, changing lifetraps is a challenging task that requires effort, persistence, and a willing-ness to risk new patterns of thinking and behaving.

As a psychological intervention, Young's ST is proving to be an effective therapeutic approach for changing lifetraps. He has identified techniques and strategies to change the thinking, feeling, behavior, and interpersonal patterns of relating that are influenced by lifetraps. At the same time, those strategies may be complemented and arguably strengthened by a host of spiritual resources available to people of faith, particularly the practice of prayer in its many forms and varieties. This psycho-spiritual approach to change is described in the remaining chapters, as a path to freedom from the fears, anxieties, and painful consequences of lifetraps.

# 2

# Praying through Lifetraps

**P**RAYER is primarily an act of relationship to God, and this relationship can assist us in recovering from the harmful effects of lifetraps on our thinking, feeling, behaving, and relating to others. There are four ways of praying that have been identified through the centuries, and each of these prayer types consists of specific strategies for change:

| Prayer Type | Spiritual Strategy for Change |
|---|---|
| *Lectio* | Taking God's perspective on yourself and your world |
| *Meditatio* | Reforming your mind and heart to that of Christ |
| *Oratio* | Conforming your will to God's will |
| *Contemplatio* | Transforming your daily experiences |

Following a brief description of these four prayer types, this chapter will focus on how each of these ways of relating to God offers unique opportunities for recovery from our lifetraps.

## Lectio

> *So shall my word be*
> *that goes forth from my mouth;*
> *It shall not return to me empty*
> *but it shall accomplish that which I purpose,*
> *and succeed in the thing for which I sent it.*
>                                   (Is 55:11)

One of the most common forms of prayer is simply to listen to the word as it speaks to us about the truth of God and reveals to us our own authentic selves. This word is communicated to us in various ways: the privileged place of Scripture, the person of Jesus, traditions or rituals, creation, books, plays, poetry, film, world events, and perhaps most poignantly through a here-and-now attention to the events of your life and God's hand at work in each of them. This listening to the word, or *Lectio* prayer, works best when we are disposed to being informed, open, and ready to receive some new information about God or ourselves.

## Meditatio

*Do not be conformed to this world, but be transformed by the renewing of your minds, so that you may discern what is the will of God, what is good and acceptable and perfect.* (Rom 12: 2)

The *Meditatio* prayer movement is all about reforming our minds to the mind of Christ, by applying our reasoning powers of imagination, memory, and understanding to our lived experience and seeing ourselves and our lives through a new lens. This meditation prayer often involves reading the Scripture with a particular focus on where you may be in the scene and how the story sheds some new light on what you have been experiencing in your life. It is usually helpful to ask for the grace of an open mind in meditation, to think beyond any preconceived ideas about God and God's role in your life or in the world. A common theme in meditation prayer is the focus on Christ's laboring for me and in me to my family, friends, and colleagues.

## Oratio

*He came out and went, as was his custom, to the Mount of Olives . . . Then he withdrew from them about a stone's throw, knelt down, and prayed, "Father, if you are willing, remove this cup from me; yet, not my will but yours be done.". . . In his anguish, he prayed more earnestly, and his sweat became like drops of blood falling down on the ground.*                                    (Lk 22:39-44)

The agony of Christ in the Garden at Gethsemane exemplifies the prayer of begging, or *Oratio*, in which we ask for the grace to conform our will to God's plan for our lives. The first step in this prayer is to discern your truest desires, and this is a difficult process of uncovering layers of desire that are less authentic—desires for safety, security, success, etc. There is certainly nothing wrong with these motives, but they often disguise a more profound interest in being at the service of God and of a larger purpose for our lives, even at the risk of personal discomfort. The prayer of oration leads to a discovery of my true self, at a certain cost, and almost inevitably to a revelation of our Christian lives as ultimately caught up in the paschal mystery—in a dying and rising to new life in the context of my own particular experience.

## Contemplatio

*As the Father has loved me, so I have loved you; abide in my love.*                                    (Jn 15:9)

The prayer of contemplation is perhaps the most profound of the four movements, as it involves a heightened and sustained awareness of God's presence and love in our lives, as well as a direct translation of that awareness into daily living. There are no new insights or revelations, no new graces for which to beg in contemplation. The focus of our contemplative prayer is simply to dwell on the awesome mystery of God in my life, knowing that we are loved and that our lives belong to God. This awareness is often sustained with the aid of holy pictures, crosses, rings, and other concrete reminders of God's fidelity to us. Perhaps more importantly, the grace of contemplation is confirmed in daily actions of love and service that flow from this heightened awareness.

## Complements to ST Change Components

This very rich tradition of prayer and its component movements can serve as a spiritual complement to the psychological interventions of Schema Therapy (ST) and as such as an invaluable resource in countering lifetraps and their noxious effects on happiness and productivity. Each of the four movements in prayer corresponds to the four major components of therapeutic change and can strengthen the psychological effectiveness of these interventions.

| Prayer Type | Spiritual Strategy | ST Strategy |
|---|---|---|
| *Lectio* | Getting a new perspective | Cognitive change |
| *Meditatio* | Identifying my heart's desires | Experiential change |
| *Oratio* | Opening myself to another | Interpersonal change |
| *Contemplatio* | Living fully in the moment | Behavioral change |

The following case illustrates how prayer can assist the ST change process across its component phases, i.e., cognitive, experiential, interpersonal, and behavioral.

## Case Example: Fear of Abandonment

Linda is a 34-year-old, single woman who has had a series of unsuccessful dating experiences and now believes that she will never find anyone suitable for marriage. Her own parents were divorced when she was eight years old, and since then she has developed a core belief that relationships are inevitably doomed to failure. In her dating experiences as an adolescent and young adult, Linda would seek out signs of impending abandonment, often when her partner would arrive late for a date, forget to carry through on something that they had agreed upon, or when he occasionally chose to spend time with friends apart from her. She would read into these events conclusive evidence that he would eventually leave her or forget about her, and she would call off the relationship to protect herself against these potential outcomes. Moreover, Linda would use these unsuccessful dating experiences as confirmation of her belief that men are not trustworthy and that relationships are doomed to end in feelings of loneliness and resentment.

## Cognitive Change and the Lectio Prayer

As previously noted, at their most surface manifestation, lifetraps are rigid and maladaptive thoughts and beliefs that distort reality and exaggerate the dangers associated with work performance and committed relationships. These cognitive distortions are informed by frustrating or traumatic early childhood experiences, and any evidence that subsequently contradicts these beliefs is selectively ignored or discounted by the lifetrapped individual. In the case of Linda, whose lifetrap is the fear of abandonment, she automatically expects that those who are initially available for support and connection will inevitably leave her or prove themselves unreliable when she needs them most. Any reassurances of love or fidelity from another are almost always minimized or dismissed in favor of this enduring and powerful belief that others cannot live up to what they are promising to deliver in the long run. Linda has remained closed off from any new evidence that might contradict her lifetrap, and she has read into any hints of unavailability the certain abandonment that will follow, even if such is far from the case.

A series of cognitive strategies may be employed to surface and dispute these distortions. First, before changing the lifetrap, it would be important to elicit all of the evidence that supports it. Anyone with Linda's insecurity about relationships and fears of abandonment might be asked to state all the reasons that support her belief that people will ultimately abandon or reject her. Then, the person working with her would counter those reasons with alternate ways of viewing that information that do not prove the lifetrap. For example, although children frequently assume responsibility for the separation or divorce of parents, it is the parents who made a mistake or were unable or unwilling to stay together. The children's anger and sadness need to be directed towards their parents and not towards themselves, as the abandonment lifetrap has mistakenly directed it.

The review of evidence that contradicts this lifetrap, a key component of any cognitive intervention, would be ordinarily comprised of positive information about you and your future prospects, and that information may profitably include the *Lectio* prayer. The word of God is replete with images, phrases, and symbols of a God who calls us beyond our fears and lifetraps, if only we allow ourselves to receive this information— often contradictory to our lifetraps—about ourselves, our relationships, and our future. For anyone struggling with fears of abandonment, you might profitably turn to reassurances

throughout the Hebrew Scriptures of God's faithful and enduring love from the moment of conception in your mother's
womb (Psalm 139), and gradually allow yourself to believe that
love need not necessarily lead to disappointment and feelings
of abandonment.

As the abandonment lifetrap has its origin in childhood
experience, individuals suffering from it may want to experience God's love as a child in the following imagery exercise.

> Picture yourself as a small child, new to this world,
> with all of the innocence and enthusiasm of childhood.
> You have no pressing concerns, no fears, and the whole
> world is excited by your arrival. You hear the sweet, soft
> sounds of loving voices; you see smiling faces doting
> over you; you are filled with peace, contentment, and joy.
> A broad smile covers your face. Now, allow the gentle
> hands of God to lift you and hold you tenderly but firm-
> ly, singing your name and rocking you lovingly in His
> arms. You see the pride in His eyes, and you hear His
> words, "I have formed you in your mother's womb, and
> you are mine" (Psalm 139).

God's love can repair feelings of abandonment and restore
faith in the enduring power of love. Spending time with scenes
like the one just described, placing yourself there as the infant
in the womb or as a young child being held by a strong, caring
adult, and allowing yourself to hear the reassuring word of
God, especially as it contradicts the core abandonment belief
about the disappointing nature of love, can soften the rigidity
of the lifetrap and prepare you for a healthier perspective on
yourself and your future. In the case of the abandonment lifetrap, a relationship with God may be the only real experience
of another who is absolutely faithful, and therefore without this

prayer component it might be more difficult, if not impossible, to begin the work of overcoming this fear.

It would be illusory to suggest that this kind of change happens in one prayer period, or even over a few. Instead, it takes repeated exposure to the evidence of love in the Word, through Scripture reading, meditation on creation, reading inspired books, and paying particular attention to the actions of God in daily life. As mentioned earlier, lifetraps are resistant to change, as they have been reinforced over years of focusing on supporting evidence and discounting any disconfirming evidence. A number of cognitive therapeutic techniques have been developed to weaken the cognitive rigidity of lifetraps.

One of these therapeutic techniques is referred to as a *Point-Counterpoint* dialogue. This exercise would have you play the role of the lifetrap, to defend its supppositions about yourself and others, while the therapist or counselor plays the role of the healthy counterpoint. This exercise is often very easy to engage, as the thoughts and feelings behind the lifetrap come so naturally to mind. Then, the roles are reversed, and you are asked to play the role of the counterpoint, while the therapist defends the positions of the lifetrap. You may learn very quickly that you are unable to defend the counterpoint very long against the persistent and convincing arguments of the lifetrap. This can be a very effective learning experience.

The *Lectio* prayer can enrich this learning experience, by permitting a confrontation with any one of the lifetraps through an argument with God about the validity of one's own deep and enduring beliefs or distortions. For those who share some of Linda's insecurity in her interpersonal relationships, you might list the reasons for finding people untrustworthy and for believing that abandonment is an inevitable outcome of every close relationship. Then counter these ideas with the multiple sayings throughout the Bible about the endurance of love. Your list might look like this:

**Abandonment is inevitable**　　**Love is everlasting**
　(your list)　　　　　　　　　　(God's list)

1. People only stay with you until the going gets tough.

1. Love bears all things, believes all things, endures all things. (1 Cor 13:7)

2. People say they love you, but they eventually show you by their actions that it's all talk.

2. Hope does not disappoint us. (Rom 5:5)

3. Why bother getting serious with anyone, when we're only going to die anyway?

3. The steadfast love of the Lord never ceases. (Lam 3:22)

First, you would argue the points on your list against those on God's list. This would likely be an easy task, as the beliefs on your list are longstanding, and you may have selected evidence to support them over many years. The heart of the exercise, however, lies in the role reversal with God. First, put your list into the mouth of God, and try to defend God's list. You may notice in relatively short order how weak and defenseless you are against the strength of the lifetrap beliefs. You simply have not invested the time or effort in taking that contrary position.

As you continue this exercise, shift your focus from your own inadequacy at defending God's list to the image of God saying the things on your list. What's wrong with this picture? Would God really defend the position that no single person deserves your trust because when the going gets tough people generally are unreliable? Can you imagine Jesus uttering these words? Or would God be afraid to commit to us because we sometimes fail to carry our words into deeds, or because we are inevitably going to die? How does God counter these arguments? Allow God to point out the weaknesses and distortions in these positions, not judgmentally but lovingly leading you to a deeper truth about yourself and others.

Another cognitive technique involves the use of a flashcard, on which the rational counterpoint to lifetraps is written out and can be consulted, particularly in moments of fear and anxiety related to any of the lifetraps. For example, you might write on your flashcard:

> *In a relationship that is grounded on open and regular communication of feelings, wants, and needs, I can trust that my partner will not suddenly abandon me or betray my trust. I will make every effort to communicate my feelings as clearly as I can and to ask for the same from my partner.*

Your flashcard can include *Lectio* material, such as assurances from God about divine love and fidelity, which can be consulted at various points in the day. For example, the use of holy cards and other concrete reminders may serve to challenge lifetrap fears and to call to mind a commitment made by the individual to amend his or her own life in more loving and productive ways. Your prayer flashcard might read:

> *There is no fear in love, but perfect love casts out fear, for fear has to do with punishment, and whoever fears has not reached perfection in love.* (1 Jn 4:18)

## Experiential Change and the Meditatio Prayer

While a significant ingredient in changing Linda's abandonment lifetrap is the naming and correcting of her distorted and self-destructive beliefs, this cognitive change component is often not enough by itself to effect a lasting change. Fueled by memories and images of real or perceived abandonment over the years, this and other lifetraps remain resistant to logical interventions — and even to the prayer interventions of the Word which offer a more hopeful and satisfying reality. The lifetrap carries with it strong emotional baggage. In Linda's case,there is anger at her frustrating experiences, as well as sadness and self-pity for her perceived fate. A second component of ST — the implementation of experiential or emotive change techniques with a special emphasis on the use of imagination—is needed to address these negative emotions and to permit their expression and transformation into more healthy, positive feelings and desires.

One of these experiential therapeutic techniques is to create an imaginary dialogue with a parent, sibling, or significant other with whom you may have experienced abandonment, loss, or betrayal:

> Start by closing your eyes and imaging that person, at the time of the unpleasant experience. Notice the details of the experience: the look on his face, the tone of his words, just what he was saying to you.

> What are you doing as he is speaking to you? What are you thinking and feeling?

> Now be the person you are today. Try to bring to mind all of the positive traits that people have ascribed to you. Relate these endearing personal traits to the one abandoning you. Tell him how you feel about how he treated you, and about the effects his treatment had on you through the years. Tell him how you would have preferred him to treat you and that you will not allow your-

self to be treated that way anymore. Tell him what you need, want, and expect from others with whom you have a significant relationship.

As you gain more experience with confronting those who betrayed or abandoned you, the lifetrap gradually weakens, and you will become more confident in your ability to state your needs and wishes for open communication, so as to minimize the risk of future sudden and unexpected loss.

A potentially useful complement to this therapeutic approach is the *Meditatio* prayer, wherein the person of faith uses the faculty of imagination to adopt a new lens on his or her lived experience. Often, people are surprised and even somewhat awkward at using imagination in prayer. However, imagination permits an interaction with God that is unscripted and tailored to the needs and wants of the individual. For example, while there may be multiple sayings in Scripture which address the fear of abandonment, the *Meditatio* prayer focuses on images to accompany those phrases, as well as the dialogue it generates.

While the therapeutic imaginary dialogue described above may afford you an opportunity to address specific individuals who hurt or betrayed you in the past, the *Meditatio* prayer is a forum for addressing the emotional baggage associated with your relationship to God. It would be hard to imagine that the anger, sadness, and self-pity that are addressed to significant others from the past are not also directed toward God. Where was God when others betrayed or abandoned me? Why didn't God protect me from that event and its emotional aftermath? These fundamental questions at the level of faith and meaning are not directly addressed with ST alone, and bringing them to the light of an imaginary dialogue within the context of *Meditatio* prayer may deepen the extent of lifetrap change.

## Meditation Prayer Experiences

Begin by selecting a passage from Scripture in which God speaks about His faithfulness and assures you that He will not leave you orphaned or abandoned. For example, you might first read the farewell discourses at the end of John's Gospel (13:33-14:31), and settle on a particular phrase for your prayer. Then close your eyes and apply each of your senses to recreate that scene, imagining yourself there listening to Jesus, noticing His eyes on you, the sound of His voice, the faces and expressions of those around you, whatever smells and tastes may surround you.

Speak to Jesus about your concerns and fears, perhaps argue with Him about what happened in your past, or simply listen to Him as He tells your story from His vantage point. Next, assume the role of one of the disciples, likewise frightened about impending abandonment and pressing Jesus for some answers, and then take the role of Jesus speaking to him or to you about these concerns and fears.

Most importantly, personalize the scene, and do not be concerned about keeping to the text, but rather use it and its images as a starting point from which to recreate a personal encounter with the Lord. You might even address Jesus as a child, expressing your early fears of abandonment, but now with the language and imagination of an adult. Through this process, you can speak directly to God about your wants and needs in a way that may have been unavailable to you at the critical time of abandonment or loss.

Another useful experiential technique is emotional catharsis which encourages individuals to verbalize unexpressed emotions that may have been ignored or pushed down for any number of reasons. People often hide their negative feelings, afraid that they may overwhelm them. Sometimes, people fear that the direct expression of their emotions, especially rage, may lead them to harm someone physically or emotionally.

Emotional catharsis is all about facilitating a more immediate awareness of these feelings and a safe forum for expressing them. For example, you might write a letter to your parents, and express in it all of the anger, sadness, disappointment, and other negative feelings that are associated with your experience of abandonment. You need not ever send the letter to your parents, although sometimes people find that empowering. Instead, it is more important simply to put those feelings into words, to externalize them, and then to share them with someone else—often a therapist or spiritual director—to receive validation for them and to assist with the important distinction between feelings that are indeed justified as opposed to those which are more lifetrap driven.

As a *Meditatio* prayer, you might write a letter to God (without mailing it, of course), expressing in it all of the feelings noted above, but this time directly to your Creator. The composition and writing of such a letter can serve as a cathartic experience, allowing you to speak to God in a way that you might otherwise have perceived as offensive or even sacrilegious. It is important to remember that God is not offended by our anger, and that there is a long tradition throughout the Hebrew Scriptures of prophets speaking directly to God about their frustration, disappointment, and disagreement with God's plan. Anyone with fears of abandonment would need encouragement to write such a letter, especially if she was afraid of divine punishment or disapproval and to help her dis-

tinguish between justifiable and unwarranted negative feelings. The exercise may also have the benefit of promoting a
more mature image of God and an adult relationship with
Him, helping one to grow beyond the passive and victimized
experience of abandonment experienced as a child and permitting a more free and comprehensive expression of the whole
range of human emotions as an adult.

## Interpersonal Change and the Oratio Prayer

Lifetraps not only lead to rigid, maladaptive cognitive distortions and restricted emotional expression, but they also
deprive our relationships of the trust and mutuality that are
essential ingredients of a healthy interpersonal life. For this reason, a person's relationships are appropriate targets for attention and change. In the context of ST, the therapeutic relationship of the individual with his or her therapist would become
the focus for this aspect of change.

Developing a healthy rapport with a therapist is necessary
to focus on the content and origins of your lifetraps and to help
you to formulate a treatment plan to change them. At the same
time, that relationship itself is not immune to lifetrap influence.
Expectations of abandonment may figure prominently in your
view of the therapist and account for fears and doubts about
that person's availability, emotional commitment, and constancy. You might find it very difficult, for example, to believe that
the therapist truly cares about you and be particularly sensitive
to changes in the schedule of meetings or to remote suggestions
that the therapist may not always be available. Clients like
Linda frequently make phone calls between sessions to test this
belief, or miss sessions to see how the therapist reacts. People
with an abandonment lifetrap may only tentatively engage in

therapy, afraid that if they fully commit to the work and to the person of the therapist, they will be ultimately disappointed and rejected.

One of the key interventions in ST is to assist you in noticing lifetrap beliefs as they emerge in the therapeutic relationship. Before any interventions are implemented to change them, these lifetraps must first be put on the table for recognition and personal responsibility. This process must often be initiated by the therapist. You might not be aware of the meaning of missed sessions nor of intersession phone calls, and the therapist's association of these behaviors with your lifetrap may at first be met with denial or dismissal. However, over time, the client notices the pattern and develops enough trust in the therapist to acknowledge these unconscious—and often embarrassing— expectations.

Once brought to awareness, the lifetrap fears are directly countered by the therapist through a process of reparenting. Being sensitive to your unmet needs for parental reassurance of emotional constancy, every effort is made to be available to you in a consistent and reliable way. This may entail offering additional sessions when you need them, or arranging for brief phone contacts between sessions to reassure you, at least implicitly, that the therapist has not forgotten you. Over time, the trust and reliability fostered in the therapy relationship will likely weaken the lifetrap of abandonment, by modeling a new way of relating that can be applied to existing and potential relationships.

While the ST therapeutic relationship can assist greatly in clarifying and satisfying unmet needs and desires, tapping into one's relationship with God can deepen an awareness of the existential fears that often underlie childhood-generated life- traps and interfere with the identification and realization of authentic desires. One may reasonably argue that unless these fears are addressed directly within the most profound relationship available to humanity, the relationship with God, they may be weakened in particular relationships but the fears themselves will continue to distract and dissuade people from living out their truest desires.

Your authentic needs and wants may be clouded and confused by the abandonment lifetrap. In the *Oratio* prayer, you encounter God as the ultimate source of meaning and existence. A fundamental assumption of this prayer movement is that, despite the circumstances leading to your lifetrap, God has a providential and loving plan for each person's life, one that is designed to fulfill your most authentic desires. St. Ignatius Loyola in *The Spiritual Exercises*—a program of prayer designed specifically to foster a relationship with God and to discern one's most authentic desires—facilitates this kind of encounter by having the individual read and reflect upon the following text which he called the "First Principle and Foundation":

*We are created to praise, reverence, and serve God our Lord, and by this means to save our souls... As far as we are concerned, we should not prefer health to sickness, riches to poverty, honor to dishonor, a long life to a short life. Our one desire and choice should be more conducive to the end for which we are created.*

You might take this passage for your *Oratio* prayer. Notice any fears and concerns that emerge as you ask for the radical grace of indifference as outlined in this First Principle and Foundation. A fear of abandonment would likely surface as an obstacle to entrusting your life so entirely to God. The *Oratio* prayer challenges you to confront the disparity between your fears and the larger vision of God for your life.

In the Garden of Gethsemane (Lk 22:39-44) Jesus models this prayer movement, as He confronts His fears and preferences in order to surrender Himself more completely to the will of God. The key ingredient in His transformation is the faithful love of God. If Jesus were not convinced that His Father was trustworthy and loving, that kind of surrender would be foolish and virtually impossible to achieve.

Our experiences of God's faithfulness, deepened by the *Lectio* and *Meditatio* prayer movements described above, are a necessary preparation for the *Oratio* experience and a constant point of reference as the anxiety of being so detached from our fears is likely to mount in this transforming prayer. It is only the conviction of God's love that permits a fundamental departure from your fear and a willingness to surrender your life so completely to His providential care.

## Behavioral Change and the Contemplatio Prayer

One of the most obvious and necessary indicators of therapeutic success is behavioral change. Until you begin to act differently, all of the insight acquired in therapy may be interesting and stimulating intellectually, but ultimately useless. All of the gains of ST and of the various prayer movements described thus far are preparation for a new way of acting in the world, one which is less dominated by lifetraps and more directed by authentic desires for your happiness and peace.

Just as the cognitive, experiential, and interpersonal components of lifetraps are explored and targeted for change, the behavioral component of the ST process focuses you on your environment, and specifically on how lifetraps have influenced a range of behaviors within that environment, e.g., kinds of romantic partners selected, family interactions, choices of work, settings. In ST, the key intervention at this stage of treatment is to challenge you to risk new behaviors that are inconsistent with lifetrap maintenance. You may be prone to avoid a romantic partner in whom you detect a serious interest, fearing that the risk of disappointment is too high. Instead, you might select a partner who is less serious about commitment, only reinforcing your abandonment lifetrap. The therapist would encourage you to stay in a relationship with a partner who is serious about commitment, even at the risk of disappointment, as a way to counter the lifetrap.

Similarly, your abandonment lifetrap may lead you to distance yourself from your parents, afraid that your unmet wants and needs may be activated by any encounter with them. Here again, you would be encouraged to risk relating to your parents, expressing your realistic wants and needs more directly, all the while prepared to deal with the possibility of disappointments.

These behavioral extensions of the gains achieved in ST would be enhanced and reinforced with the *Contemplatio* prayer. While the commitment to live according to one's authentic desires and divine destiny is the primary grace sought in the *Oratio* prayer, the *Contemplatio* prayer is all about living that grace in your daily life. It would be essential to notice the evidences of God's love and His multiple invitations to abandon your fears and surrender to Him. As an antidote to your abandonment lifetrap, you would be encouraged to take notice of God's faithful love in your present relationships, family, work experiences, and the many interactions that comprise each day. You might take ten or fifteen minutes daily to examine your day for this kind of evidence, and then to contemplate appropriate responses. In the end, you might take some of the same risks targeted by ST, but for a larger purpose, namely to live according to a divine plan for your life. And that motivation for behavioral change may make all the difference!

In the chapters of the next section of this book, specific lifetrap patterns will be targeted for consideration, with a focus on how to treat them from this psycho-spiritual perspective. Various spiritual resources will be considered, including meditation, mindfulness, journaling, detachment, and surrender. You may choose to engage in these spiritual practices either in the context of professional counseling, spiritual direction, or simply on your own through spiritual reading. The last section of this book will describe and differentiate each of these modalities for your consideration.

# Part II

# Lifetrap Patterns and
# Psycho-Spiritual Recovery

NOW that you have had an opportunity to read in general terms about the lifetraps and perhaps to identify one or more of your own, you are ready to use the prayer techniques described in Chapter 2 to find more freedom and happiness in your life.

Each of the chapters in Part II will focus on a specific lifetrap pattern—including the ways of thinking, feeling, behaving, and relating to others that are unique to that lifetrap theme—and ways to alter these toxic themes with therapeutic and spiritual strategies. This is the core of psycho-spiritual recovery.

You may notice aspects of yourself in one, some, or maybe even all of the lifetrap chapters that follow. It is important for you to take from each of the respective chapters the strategies and techniques that will be useful to you. Remember that this is a book about recovery, not about feeling bad or defective because you find yourself identified with some or many of these lifetraps. Committing yourself to growth in truth and holiness is the goal, not making yourself perfect.

Following an application of this psycho-spiritual approach to each of the lifetrap themes, Part III of this book will point you in the direction of some resources that might assist you as you continue your journey toward greater freedom.

# 3

# Don't Get Too Close to Me

FOR some people, the world of social interactions is a very threatening place. Instead of finding comfort, humor, ease, and warmth in the company of family, friends, and work associates, you may experience yourself as more detached from social relationships, perhaps freezing up in interpersonal settings or simply avoiding them altogether to protect yourself from those uncomfortable feelings. As a result, you may end up without any close friends or confidants, and left alone with your anger and resentment. Or worse, you may become overly suspicious of the intentions of others, believing that they are ultimately out to deceive and harm you. You may be harboring grudges, unwilling to accept that others are capable of sincerity in their contrition and in making amends. Forgiveness may seem impossible, and probably not even desirable. You have learned to value your self-sufficiency above all else and have built up an impermeable wall around your heart.

From a lifetrap perspective, you may be under the influence of those rigid beliefs associated with early childhood experiences of disconnection and rejection (*abandonment, emotional deprivation, mistrust*). Rate the following statements that are designed to measure each of these lifetraps, adapted from the Young Schema Questionnaire, by using the scoring key to determine how much you believe each of them is true of you.

## Scoring Key

1   Completely untrue of me
2   Mostly untrue of me
3   Slightly more true than untrue of me
4   Moderately true of me
5   Mostly true of me
6   Describes me perfectly

## Abandonment Questionnaire

_____ 1. I am preoccupied with losing the significant people in my life.

_____ 2. I often worry about being left alone.

_____ 3. I am afraid that significant people in my life will ultimately abandon me.

_____ 4. I worry that I won't be able to rely on anyone for emotional support.

_____ 5. I don't feel that important relationships will last; I expect them to end.

_____ 6. I always seem to get attached to partners who are unreliable.

_____ 7. It seems that the important people in my life are always coming and going.

_____ 8. When I feel someone distancing from me, I get even more clingy.

_____ 9. Sometimes I can't hide how much I am worried about people leaving me.

_____10. I become upset when someone isn't in contact with me, even for a short period of time.

_____**Your Total Score on Abandonment**
     (Add your scores for statements 1-10)

## Emotional Deprivation Questionnaire

_____ 1. I am constantly looking for more love and support in my life.

_____ 2. I have never found someone who really appreciates what I am feeling.

_____ 3. Many of my relationships are with unemotional people.

_____ 4. I feel emotionally detached from most people

_____ 5. I have never had a satisfying intimate relationship with anyone.

_____ 6. I have rarely had the closeness and tenderness that I long for.

_____ 7. People generally are not able to show me empathy.

_____ 8. I block others from getting close to me.

_____ 9. I have never had enough love and attention.

_____10. I often feel isolated and misunderstood.

_____**Your Total Score on Emotional Deprivation**
     (Add your scores for statements 1-10)

## Mistrust and Abuse Questionnaire

_____ 1. I believe that people will take advantage of me if I give them the chance.

____ 2. Friends will betray you.

____ 3. People are never completely honest with what they are thinking.

____ 4. I have to stay suspicious of others, or else I'll be hurt.

____ 5. People misinterpret kindness for weakness.

____ 6. I look for proof that people are well-intentioned.

____ 7. Self-defense is my first priority.

____ 8. It's dangerous to trust anyone.

____ 9. I can't forgive those who have really hurt me.

____10. I have been mistreated or neglected by important people in my life.

____**Your Total Score on Mistrust and Abuse**
(Add your scores for statements 1-10)

### Interpreting Your Lifetrap Total Scores

| | | |
|---|---|---|
| 10-19 | Very low | This lifetrap probably does not apply to you. |
| 20-29 | Fairly low | This lifetrap may only apply occasionally. |
| 30-39 | Moderate | This lifetrap is an issue in your life. |
| 40-49 | High | This is an important lifetrap for you. |
| 50-60 | Very high | This is one of your core lifetraps. |

If your family of origin was detached, cold, withholding, or abusive, then you have probably learned to see the world of human interactions as threatening and undesirable. You may be afraid of abandonment, or believe that people are ultimately incapable of meeting your needs for emotional reliability and support. If you experienced physical, emotional, or sexual abuse as a child, it would not be surprising for you to believe now that anyone is likely to hurt or take advantage of you, perhaps especially those who ought to be close to you.

The core problem underlying these lifetraps is, of course, the fear and isolation that results from the perception of extreme vulnerability in interpersonal interactions. Unfortunately, this kind of experience is not uncommon in our society. Sherry Turkle, a professor at MIT, wrote in *Science, Technology, and Society:* "Terrified of being alone, yet afraid of intimacy, we experience widespread feelings of emptiness, of disconnection, of the unreality of self. And here the computer, a companion without emotional demands, offers a compromise. You can be a loner, but never alone. You can interact, but need never feel vulnerable to another person." In our computer age, people are flocking to chat rooms, where anonymity and protection from emotional vulnerability are kept closely in check.

If these lifetraps are walling you in emotionally, how do you get out? Where do you start? First, it is important to do a thorough self-examination to determine the extent to which these lifetraps may be influencing your life. The first goal in recovery from any of these lifetraps is to develop an appropriate sense of self-awareness. Are you so used to being a loner that you have become largely unaware of your own feelings toward others, especially the anger and resentment that you bear? Or are you too aware of others and so focused on any hints of unreliability or potential for manipulation and deceit on their part that you minimize or ignore your own bitter feelings and their toxic effects on others? Once you have fostered a heightened sense of self-awareness, the second goal is to develop ease in communicating those feelings to others, a task that has been no doubt avoided at all cost up to this point. Psychological and spiritual resources are useful tools in meeting these goals of lifetrap recovery.

## Becoming Self-aware

Perhaps the best way to start, one that would not require immediate interaction with others but that would gradually prepare for such encounters, may be the use of a journal. Writing down your thoughts and feelings on a daily basis, even for only ten minutes a day, can serve as a safe and effective means of paying attention to yourself. Remember that you are not doing this for anyone else. No one will judge, misunderstand, or use that information against you. Many studies have shown that recording feelings may improve physical health, enhance immune function, reduce cardiovascular reactivity, and even prolong your life.

Another useful spiritual resource is the practice of centering prayer as a means of strengthening self-awareness. It delivers the physical and emotional benefits described above with journaling, and studies have shown that this kind of prayer relieves stress, bolsters self-esteem, and reduces symptoms of anxiety and depression. Centering prayer is not designed to be an end in itself, but rather to facilitate the prayer methods described in the last chapter. Thomas Keating, in his *Intimacy with God*, offers a helpful method for engaging in centering prayer, to be practiced daily, preferably for a minimum of twenty to thirty minutes, twice a day:

1. Choose a sacred word as a symbol of your intention to open and yield to God's presence and action within. It could be one of the names of God or a comforting word, such as presence, silence, peace, stillness.

2. Sit comfortably and with eyes closed, relax. Then silently introduce the sacred word as the symbol of one's consent to God's presence and action within.

3. During the prayer time, avoid analyzing the experience or harboring expectations to achieve any specific goal.

4.  At the end of the prayer time, remain in silence with eyes closed for a short time, allowing the psyche a brief space to readjust to the external senses and to transfer the atmosphere of interior silence into subsequent activities.

This kind of exercise is designed to focus your awareness and to improve your powers of concentration, and so to serve as an antidote to the emotional numbness created by the disconnected lifetraps. As you become more comfortable with yourself, you may experience an inner sense of peace, joy, and well-being, and over time come to appreciate the transcendent interconnectedness that exists among human beings. This awareness will likely set the stage for communicating your feelings to others.

Still another spiritual practice that is related to centering prayer and is the basis for the kinds of prayer described in the last chapter is mindfulness. Rather than judging or trying to control your fears or negative expectations of others, mindful awareness helps to cultivate an attitude of acceptance. You simply focus on what you are thinking, feeling, experiencing in the present moment, trying not to block the feelings or change them. It's like letting the wave of your thoughts and emotions, images and perceptions pass over you, reaching a crescendo and then falling on their own.

This kind of experience may soften the anger and frustration that frequently accompanies feelings of disconnection and rejection. Practicing mindfulness may help you to tolerate those fears long enough to appreciate that they are not in charge of your life, even though they may exercise an inordinate amount of influence on your attitudes and behavior toward others. *You* are not the tidal wave of fears and preoccupations with abandonment or abuse; instead, these fears are holding you captive and their intensity can wax and wane. The more that you cultivate this awareness of lifetrap fears as separate powerful forces that can harm but not destroy you, the more empowered you will feel to engage in the strategies practiced in ST and in the prayer options described in the last chapter.

In his book, *Spirituality In Clinical Practice*, Len Sperry outlines four steps in the daily practice of mindfulness:

1.  Set aside 20 minutes and choose an activity like walking, watching, or listening to music.
2.  Try to be totally present to that activity for the 20-minute time frame. For example, if you are out walking, focus on a particular object, e.g., tree, flower, child playing, etc.
3.  Let your thoughts and feelings surface and simply notice them, again without trying to censor or change them. Perhaps you will notice that you are connected to nature, or to humanity, in a way that you had not really noticed before. Just be with those thoughts and feelings.
4.  Try to carry those feelings of centeredness and belonging into your next daily activity.

## Communicating Your Feelings

Once you have practiced some of these exercises designed to heighten your sense of self-awareness, you are better prepared to communicate those feelings to others. As your sense of self-awareness and self-possession increases, you are more likely to dispel the isolation associated with the disconnection lifetraps and to believe that your thoughts and feelings are worthy of attention, respect, and understanding. You may also discover a new sense of spiritual connectedness to nature, other human beings, and to God. This sense of connectedness is precisely the antidote to the lifetraps of disconnection and rejection, and the necessary starting point for the practice of self-disclosure.

Because the disconnection lifetraps may have convinced you that your feelings are likely to be ignored, misunderstood, or used against you, you may automatically go on the offensive. Instead of telling others how you feel when you are upset or disappointed, you may be more likely to point out their faults and to attack or dismiss them outright. The likely outcome of such encounters, of course, is that you are then actually rejected, and the lifetrap is only reinforced.

Ornish, in his *Love and Survival,* proposes an exercise in communicating feelings that may be helpful in recognizing experientially the difference between expressing critical thoughts and the disclosure of feelings. You might try to do this exercise with a trusted friend, confidant, therapist, or spiritual director. That person will give you the following instructions:

- Close your eyes. Take a deep breath. Get comfortable. Center yourself. Pay attention to how you feel when I say:

  **"I think you are wrong! And I think you're a jerk!"**

- Okay. Open your eyes. How did that feel? Notice all the feelings and sensations that you experienced in that moment. You probably felt attacked, judged, angry, upset, etc. The most common responses to these feelings are withdrawal or counter-attack.

- Now close your eyes again. Take a deep breath. Get comfortable. Center yourself. Pay attention to how you feel when I say :

  **"I feel angry. I feel upset."**

- Okay. Open your eyes again. Was it the same or different? Notice all the feelings and sensations that you experienced in that moment. Perhaps you felt a more open heart, because you cannot argue with feelings; they are simply true. This feeling expression usually invites the other person into the experience, rather than pushing them away.

This kind of exercise may complement the ST experiential techniques that are designed to foster a freer expression of feelings in the context of the helping relationship. As you gain experience in directly communicating your feelings with a trusted friend or helper, without fear of reprisal or rejection, you may begin to extend this practice to other appropriate people in your life, becoming more confident, over time, that you and your feelings are indeed worthy of attention and understanding.

# 4

# Help! I Can't Handle Life on My Own

HAVE you ever wanted to make a change at work, perhaps to take on new responsibilities that would advance your career and add some excitement and creativity to your labor, but you were afraid that you would get into something that you might not be able to handle or succeed at without considerable help from others? Do you experience the ordinary responsibilities of taking care of children, managing your household, or balancing your budget as insurmountable tasks? Do you need to get the opinion of at least ten others before you decide to go on that date or take that trip you've been talking about for the past several months? Is it really difficult for you to be alone? Do you fill your weekends with appointments and dates? If you break up with your boyfriend, do you feel the need to replace him immediately, or even to have the next person in place before the break-up—all to avoid being alone?

If you answered yes to one or more of the above questions, your happiness and freedom may be compromised by the *dependence* lifetrap. Rate the following statements that are designed to measure this lifetrap, taken from the Young Schema Questionnaire, by using the scoring key to determine how much you believe each of them is true of you.

## Scoring Key

1   Completely untrue of me
2   Mostly untrue of me
3   Slightly more true than untrue of me
4   Moderately true of me
5   Mostly true of me
6   Describes me perfectly

## Dependence Questionnaire

_____ 1. I feel incompetent in handling ordinary tasks.

_____ 2. I am always looking for others to help me achieve my goals.

_____ 3. I have a hard time dealing with stress on my own.

_____ 4. Other people seem to know my needs better than I.

_____ 5. I am always seeking guidance when it comes to making a new decision.

_____ 6. It seems like I always mess up things I do on my own.

_____ 7. My judgment is poor.

_____ 8. I don't have the ability to figure things out on my own.

_____ 9. I am very reluctant to rely on my skills or initiative.

_____10. I need a lot of help to deal with daily responsibilities.

_____**Your Total Score on Dependence**

(Add your scores for statements 1-10)

## Interpreting Your Lifetrap Total Score

10-19   Very low      This lifetrap probably does not apply to you.
20-29   Fairly low    This lifetrap may only apply occasionally.

30-39     Moderate     This lifetrap is an issue in your life.

40-49     High         This is an important lifetrap for you.

50-60     Very high    This is one of your core lifetraps.

According to Young, if you have this *dependence* lifetrap, then you probably believe that you are unable to handle everyday responsibilities without considerable help from others, and so you often appear helpless. Moreover, this sense of helplessness is frequently accompanied by considerable anger and frustration over holding yourself back from attaining success at work and love. You may turn that anger against yourself, deeply resenting your intransigent sense of helplessness, or experience anger at others who never seem as available or helpful as you think they should be.

Young proposes that the typical family origin for this lifetrap is overprotective parenting. In the normal course of development, a child is gradually permitted more and more freedom to try new things on her own, to separate from her primary caretaker, and to be rewarded and praised for her independent accomplishments. If you developed the dependence lifetrap, you probably learned from your parents that you were ill-equipped to try new things on your own, or that the world was too complicated or dangerous to permit you safely and successfully to try something new without your parents' direct participation. This kind of parenting undermined your developing sense of self-confidence and makes you reluctant as an adult to take the kinds of risks that are necessary to achieve success in your work and relationships.

From a psycho-spiritual perspective, there are at least two prominent goals for changing this lifetrap: (1) to increase your sense of self-sufficiency and readiness to engage life just as you are, with all of your limitations and assets; and (2) to take more risks at work and at home without always waiting for the permission or assistance of others.

## Increasing Self-confidence

You may be used to weighing your limitations too heavily, always considering how you may fail without someone's help. You may think that you are not intelligent or skilled enough to complete a particular task. If you have boxed in your personal and professional life around these perceived limitations, you may now be afraid to take steps out of those boxes. You are lifetrapped by a pervasive sense of dependency that has undermined your self-confidence.

In order to restore that self-confidence, you first need to evaluate your judgments about your competence and limitations. One of the techniques of ST is to review the evidence for and against these beliefs. With the assistance of a therapist or another helping person you may be challenged to consider alternative thoughts that are closer to the truth. For example, you might be reassured that you—like all people—have certain limitations, but that these are points for consideration and not reasons to avoid challenges. Successful people are not without limitations. You may be invited to focus on a historical, political, or family figure who, despite their limitations—or maybe even because of them—has risen to life challenges successfully.

As a spiritual resource, you may want to turn to *Lectio* prayer experiences, perhaps by reading about biblical figures like the prophet Jeremiah, who initially protested against his call because he was too young to take on the role of a prophet. God responded that he was to serve just as he was, without waiting for age or experience to sharpen his skills or equip him with the requisite maturity for the task of prophecy. The apostle Peter was likewise reluctant to accept the call to ministry, asking Jesus to leave him, a sinful man. Jesus did not wait for Peter to become a more holy man; instead, he called him to follow Him as he was, confused, weak and arguably less than ideally suited for apostleship.

You may follow these readings with some *Lectio* imagery exercises, allowing God to speak to you as a child who is afraid to step out on your own, perhaps to ride that bicycle, join that new group, or start that new project. Let God reassure and encourage you by letting you know that He is with you whatever the task or challenge. Alternatively, you may visualize Him standing across the stormy sea with arms outstretched, waiting to catch you if you fall but inviting you to walk to Him on your own.

Of course, the process of changing lifetraps is not only a matter of changing your thoughts but of expressing your dependency fears and related negative emotions more directly. In the case of the dependence lifetrap, the underlying emotion is often one of intense anger at feeling so helpless at meeting life's challenges on your own. Spiritual resources can be very helpful in assisting this therapeutic process. You may want to express that anger in a *Meditatio* prayer experience, through an imaginary dialogue with God, or by writing a letter to God, telling Him how angry and frustrated you are with these enduring fears. In most of your significant relationships, you are too afraid to speak your mind openly, and your stance is often one of submissiveness because you do not want to risk losing these essential relationships in your life.

This relational pattern only strengthens your dependence lifetrap beliefs. With God, however, you have the opportunity to speak openly because you are assured in faith that He will never abandon you, no matter how angry you are or how much you disagree with His plan. God is committed to your growth in freedom, and a healthy parenting style permits you to say no, to take risks, and to learn from your choices without fear or guilt. You can write or speak freely about your real desires without the extraordinary fear of failure that has accompanied your independent strivings in life.

These changes in self-perception and emotional expression are essential components of increasing self-confidence, and they prepare the way for a life that is less dependent on the approval or assistance of others.

## Taking Risks

In order to confront and alter the fear of being alone that underlies this lifetrap, you would be well-advised to work with a therapist, counselor, pastor, or some other helper to establish a list of tasks to accomplish on your own. You might start out with the less risky tasks of spending time alone in prayer or spiritual reading, as these are not likely to have any adverse consequences. It is important for you to spend the time alone and not to compromise that time with other activities that would put you in touch with others. Gradually, as your comfort in being alone is strengthened, you might start to take on some independent projects, again starting with one in which you feel free enough to make mistakes. Ideally, this would not be something for public scrutiny but a personal work, such as a writing or art project, or making some long-range plans for your business or career. Eventually, you may want to initiate something that would have more public consequences, starting with the one with the least negative possibilities.

A similar behavioral strategy can be used with your interpersonal relationships. You may want to practice spending some time alone without scheduling any activities. Spend the time reading, listening to music, or doing anything that you can do alone. You may need a lot of encouragement at first to do this, as your dependence lifetrap insists that you are vulnerable if left alone and incapable of doing something constructive. Gradually, you may take some more public risks, perhaps going to the movies or out to dinner on your own. Your goal is to rely more on your instincts to let you know what you need, rather than on the ideas of others. This new attitude will free you to make choices about how to spend your time and energy and may not meet with everyone's approval. In time you will learn that your life is your own, and that you are well prepared to direct it as you will, with the assurance of God's grace.

# 5

# Me First!

$\mathcal{J}\underline{\underline{*}}$

HAVE you ever pushed your way ahead of others to buy a ticket or purchase groceries in a long line, assuming that your time is more valuable or that you are less able to handle the wait than others? Do you get offended when your requests for service are not immediately satisfied? Do you need to have answers to your questions without delay? Does it bother you when you are asked to give additional information before you receive an answer?

If you answered affirmatively to any of the above questions, you may be unduly influenced by the *entitlement* lifetrap. Rate the following statements that are designed to measure this lifetrap, again taken from the Young Schema Questionnaire, by using the scoring key to determine how much you believe each of them is true of you.

## Scoring Key

1   Completely untrue of me
2   Mostly untrue of me
3   Slightly more true than untrue of me
4   Moderately true of me
5   Mostly true of me
6   Describes me perfectly

## Entitlement Questionnaire

_____ 1. I don't handle disappointments well.

_____ 2. I get very angry when people or circumstances frustrate my plans.

_____ 3. I often seek ways to get around the normal rules and regulations that govern most people.

_____ 4. My own wishes come before those of others.

_____ 5. It's hard for me to give up things that I enjoy, even when I know they're bad for me.

_____ 6. I can't sustain interest in ordinary tasks.

_____ 7. I lose my temper very easily.

_____ 8. I usually abandon tasks that require a great deal of patience and persistence.

_____ 9. People who work with me or for me should follow my direction at all times.

_____10. I often act impulsively.

_____**Your Total Score on Entitlement**
> (Add your scores for statements 1-10)

## Interpreting Your Lifetrap Total Score

| | | |
|---|---|---|
| 10-19 | Very low | This lifetrap probably does not apply to you. |
| 20-29 | Fairly low | This lifetrap may only apply occasionally. |
| 30-39 | Moderate | This lifetrap is an issue in your life. |
| 40-49 | High | This is an important lifetrap for you. |
| 50-60 | Very high | This is one of your core lifetraps. |

Young describes this lifetrap as the belief that you are superior to other people and are not bound by the rules of reciprocity that guide normal social interaction. You may think you are more powerful, intelligent, or successful than others, even though you are not aware that you think this way. As a result, you may experience an excessive need for admiration and praise, and you are likely to ignore the needs or feelings of others, focusing on your own wishes and how to meet them as expeditiously and thoroughly as possible. You first!

Unlike the other lifetraps, people with the entitlement lifetrap are less aware of the negative consequences of this lifetrap on their emotional well-being or interpersonal relationships. Trapped, as it were, in their own self-absorption, entitled individuals are also less likely to seek help in overcoming this lifetrap. After all, people with the entitlement lifetrap can be successful in their endeavors, at least for a while, although there are inevitable problems that arise because of it. For example, their excessive need for admiration may over time alienate even their most devoted friends and associates. Len Sperry claims that the narcissistic personality, arguably just another name for people with the entitlement lifetrap, inevitably drives others away, because as time goes by, their personal presence seems less genuine to others, "having a gamey quality to it."

The childhood origins of this lifetrap, according to Young, lay in a parental failure to set appropriate limits for the child. They fail to teach the child how to tolerate having his wishes delayed or denied and that the rights and desires of others are as important as his. A family atmosphere of permissiveness and overindulgence fosters the entitlement lifetrap and is itself a form of emotional deprivation—as realistic limits are an essential developmental need for all children. Consequently, the child grows up with an outward presentation of power and control that is shallow because the underlying feelings are of deprivation and emptiness. That is the essential paradox of entitled individuals, and the reason that they can be so easily insulted and reduced to despondency. Their inner sense of resilience is weak, perhaps non-existent, and so they interpret even the ordinary frustrations of life as radical assaults on their self-esteem. Moreover, because they have not been taught as children to tolerate frustrations and disappointments, these injuries may engender overwhelming feelings of despair, anger, sadness, and hopelessness. Entitled people are prone to turn to alcohol, drugs, or other addictive behaviors to medicate these feelings and to re-establish the control that is otherwise so fragile in their lives.

From a ST perspective, one might argue that the core problem with the entitlement lifetrap is the preoccupation with control. The unhealthy thoughts, feelings, behaviors, and interpersonal relationships associated with this lifetrap all surface from the core perceived need for mastery and control in all circumstances and at all expense. This preoccupation with control is at the heart of all addictive processes, and while the entitlement lifetrap may not be the exclusive avenue to the development of an addiction, it certainly puts one at risk for this kind of behavior. In view of this, the remaining section of this chapter will focus on the nature of addictive behaviors, and how entitled individuals may be especially prone to them. We will also see how to use spiritual means to recognize and recover from the control-seeking that drives them.

## Am I an Addict?

Gerald May defines addiction as an "unholy attachment." Looking beyond the substances of alcohol, drugs, food, etc.,

May focuses on the processes that characterize addictions, i.e., inordinate attachments to certain things or relationships, and points out that these addictions and the security that they promise are ultimately inadequate substitutes for God. May identifies five essential characteristics of all addictive processes: (1) tolerance; (2) withdrawal; (3) self-deception; (4) loss of willpower; and (5) distortion of attention.

*Tolerance* is a process that is described extensively in substance abuse literature. It means that you need more and more of a particular substance over time to achieve the desired effect. If you are an alcoholic, you will need more alcohol to get drunk as your addiction advances than when you first started drinking. Thus, it is alarming to hear someone proudly confess that they can hold their liquor better than others, as this usually means that they have developed a higher tolerance and that their problem is more severe.

As an addictive process, tolerance is insidious, often unnoticed and frequently minimized by the addict. For example, you may not be aware that your need for money is addictive, until you stop to think about whether you need more and more over time, to get the desired effect of feeling happy or secure. For the entitled individual, tolerance is especially problematic, as they can never get enough power, control, or praise to feel secure. Plagued by deep-seated feelings of emptiness and an endless pursuit of admiration, your closest friends are put to the loyalty test and their attention is often found wanting. You may be addicted to relationships, using them to satisfy your hunger for security, but ultimately feel disappointed and frustrated by their limitations. To determine if you are caught in this lifetrap, ask yourself: Do I have enough power, control, and success in my life to feel secure? Am I always seeking more and more attention, recognition, praise, and never able to feel satisfied for very long when I attain it?

Another component of the addictive process is *withdrawal*. Just as with alcohol or heroin addiction, where the person experiences extremely unpleasant physical and psychological effects when they cease using the substance, so too with addictions or attachments to relationships. If you try to stop using others and attempt to reach out and give selflessly, you will initially experience some emotional pain. Because you labor under the entitlement lifetrap, you may experience the shift of focus away from yourself and toward someone else as excessively burdensome. This awareness may occasion anxiety, anger, and perhaps a physical or emotional distancing from the other person. Or if you are addicted to someone else's approval, then when they criticize you, even if appropriately and graciously, you will likely experience emotional withdrawal symptoms accompanying the temporary absence of praise. These may include considerable stress and feelings of emptiness, loneliness, and deprivation. To check yourself, ask: If I were to lose the praise and admiration of others, or of one person in particular, even temporarily, how would I feel? If you think the emotional consequences would be akin to the ones described above, or if you ever actually experienced these emotions in response to some perceived loss of attention or approval, then you are likely to be addicted to that relationship.

*Self-deception* is another hallmark of addictive processes. Denial is one of the most prominent tools of self-deception. The addict will simply not see the problem, or minimize its severity or effect in his life and may rationalize his behavior (e.g., everyone is doing it) or else blame others for their behavior (e.g., if I don't put myself first, then others will take advantage of me). While the more obvious manifestation of the entitlement lifetrap is the manipulation of others, the entitled person may also engage in self-deception, either by denying how much they depend on others for admiration or by excusing their manipulative behavior by blaming an exploitative, dog-eat-dog world. Ask yourself: Do I make excuses for manipulating others or pushing others out of the way so that I can be first? Maybe you are addicted to competing with others to protect yourself from acknowledging more directly your need for emotional support.

Sooner or later, everyone who engages in addictive processes experiences a *loss of willpower*—they continue to engage in the addictive behavior, despite efforts to stop. This is the hallmark of dependence, as it is defined in the *Diagnostic and Statistical Manual of Mental Disorders* (DSM-IV). Inevitably, you will experience significant stressors in life that may challenge your attachment to control, e.g., aging, illness, career setbacks, divorce, death of a loved one, and you may be ready to acknowledge that life is ultimately beyond your control. You may be willing to surrender that attachment, but it is likely that feelings of emptiness and deprivation will surface and you will not be able to bear them without substituting another person or substance to control. If you find yourself in this position, then you have convincing evidence that you are addicted to control.

Among all of these signposts of addiction, perhaps the most self-damaging is the *distortion of attention* from love. If you are preoccupied with obtaining the substance or relationship, in order to secure the desired effects (control, euphoria, security), then your attention is kidnapped, according to May, hindering your capacity for love. For the entitled individual, the addictive need for admiration— to be praised, satisfied, and always in a position of superiority over others—precludes the experience of real love for others, God, and self. Fundamentally, the addiction to control is a displacement of a spiritual hunger. In other words, you may be trying to fulfill your longing for God through these attachments to things or persons over which you exercise control or mastery. Because the quest for God involves the uncomfortable risk of being vulnerable—of surrendering power, security, and control—you prefer instead to settle for lesser gods, with whom your illusion of control is less threatened. Spiritual recovery from the entitlement lifetrap and the addiction to control that underlies it, therefore, entails a radical transformation of your desires, from the quest for mastery to a commitment to self-surrender.

## Recovering from the Addiction to Control

Since one of the key characteristics of the entitlement lifetrap is an inability to tolerate frustration and disappointment, the ST cognitive interventions necessarily focus on teaching you to cope more adaptively with life stressors and with the limitations of others. Your challenge would be to balance your needs with the needs of others, to follow the rules, and to challenge your perception that you ought to have special rights and privileges. A focus on religious coping can be particularly useful in assisting this process of change.

Ken Pargament has identified four predominant religious coping styles: (1) self-directing; (2) collaborative; (3) deferring; and (4) pleading. The s*elf-directing* style dictates that even if you believe in God, you see yourself as having the responsibility to deal with your feelings and take actions on your own, without God's help. The *collaborative* style, on the other hand, approaches God as a partner in the coping process, to find meaning in difficult situations, implement solutions to problems, and to sustain yourself emotionally. The *deferring* approach puts the problem entirely in God's hands, and the *pleading* style bargains with God to make things better.

Pargament points out that the collaborative style is most associated with good physical health and emotional well-being. For the entitled individual to cultivate this approach to God would entail a thorough and honest assessment of how truly dependent you are on God. This would likely bring you very close to the experience of emptiness, but instead of leaving you there, the *Lectio* material that was employed for those with emotional deprivation lifetraps might be useful again here, e.g., "I am with you always." The more that you experience God's steady, reliable love, the less likely you are to turn to controlling others to secure positive feelings about yourself. Moreover, the collaborative religious coping style emphasizes the equal partnership that you share with God, and this union will likely reduce the extent to which you may feel threatened by the limits and frustrations that are an inevitable part of life.

Spiritual surrender means doing your best and then turning the rest into God's hands. It involves an openness to recognize a higher value in seemingly negative situations. For example, when you are disappointed, rather than force your way or react with rage, you would ask the question: What am I supposed to learn in this situation? From a spiritual perspective, it is not my own wishes and desires that have the final say, but God's will for me. Twelve-Step programs are founded on this simple spiritual message—simple, but not easy.

Spiritual surrender in these situations involves the experience of self-transcendence, going from "playing God" to "seeking God." Over time, you can transform your perspective from one of seeing yourself as the center of the world to seeing God there. This surrender is almost always accompanied by an enhanced state of well-being, characterized by feelings of completeness, serenity, and compassion. Pargament reports that spiritual surrender has accounted for lower depression, better quality of life, and growth in dealing with stress.

From a theological perspective, spiritual surrender is a response to grace—the constant, unwavering love of God. People do not surrender to a distant God. The experience of God's sustaining and delivering you, in ways that are unexpected or beyond your control, even when your attention is distorted or your willpower is compromised by your addiction to control, are invaluable ingredients in your recovery from this lifetrap.

The Twelve-Step tradition has offered numerous pathways to increase a sense of God's presence and to assist in coping with life stressors and in surrendering control. Perhaps the clearest and most obvious antidote to the entitlement lifetrap is the cultivation of the virtue of humility. Humility is an accurate sense of one's self-importance. There are some key steps to humility that are highlighted in the formal Twelve Steps:

1. (Step 1) You must have a core spiritual belief in an external, transcendent power who is all-knowing and all-powerful. You can develop this sense by engaging in *Lectio* prayer using relevant Scripture passages like Psalm 139, where you focus on God who has the whole universe, time itself, and your very life in the palm of His hands.

2. (Step 5) This step recommends that you consider your misdeeds and wrongdoings by way of a personal inventory. It is not enough to write down these deeds for yourself—although that is a necessary precursor (Step 4)—but to cultivate a deeper awareness of your vulnerabilities, precisely by sharing them with someone else. In ST, this sharing is done with your therapist confronting your entitlement and supporting your expression of vulnerability. This experi-

ence would likely have the twofold benefit of: (1) modeling a new way of coping with stress, and (2) teaching you that you do not have to maintain control in all situations—that vulnerability is not defeat. You may want to prepare for this actual sharing with someone else, whether in a professional or informal context, by first sharing with God through *Meditatio* prayer experiences. Using imagery to encounter the living God who welcomes you, warts and all, and who continues to love you even after you express your misdeeds, can enhance your readiness to recreate that encounter with someone else.

3.  (Step 10) This step encourages you to make amends for your misdeeds. This emphasis on behavioral change is consistent with the ST insistence that the proof of change is in your new pattern of acting. By approaching those in your life whom you may have injured by your attempts to put yourself first, you are weakening the unnecessary sense of superiority that has guided your entitlement lifetrap.

Other spiritual virtues that may be useful in overcoming the addiction to control are serenity and gratitude. These may be enhanced by *Contemplatio* prayer experiences, simply by reciting a phrase (e.g., the Serenity Prayer, "God grant me the serenity to accept the things I cannot change"), or by simply noticing in the daily details of your life the real evidence that God is in control and is continually giving you all that you need in each moment. It is interesting to note that when you are feeling most entitled, and more ready than ever to push and shove other people out of your way to accomplish your agenda, there is little or no gratitude in your heart. You have forgotten to notice the many gifts all around you and to express your gratitude to God. Simply by stopping to say "thank you" to God periodically throughout your day will go a long way toward combating your compulsive need for control and will assist you in slowing down long enough to live a more healthy and balanced life.

Perhaps the greatest tonic in overcoming the entitlement lifetrap is the practice of forgiveness. Len Sperry suggests that, next to prayer, forgiveness may be the most commonly practiced spiritual experience. Robert Enright points out that forgiveness, defined as "a willingness to abandon one's right to resentment, negative judgment, and indifferent behavior toward one who unjustly injures us," is rooted in all world religions. There are certainly numerous studies of the effects of forgiveness on health and emotional well-being, and they all suggest that forgiveness is beneficial to the one who extends it. This is a key insight for the entitled person, who is more inclined to believe that he will lose his superior status if he offers forgiveness to those who have injured his fragile self-esteem. Sperry has reviewed existing protocols for letting go of anger and for extending forgiveness, and he summarizes the guidelines offered by Cynthia Sanderson and Marsha Linehan:

1. Consider the pros and cons of forgiving the person versus not forgiving the person, including the effects of one's anger on one's psychological and physical health.

2. Use cognitive reframing to understand the offending person's behavior.

3. If the offending person is sincerely sorry, practice validation of his or her distress.

4. Act opposite to angry feelings by engaging in conciliatory behavior.

These guidelines correspond closely to the ST cognitive strategies for entitlement, where the negative consequences of this lifetrap on your health and well-being are highlighted (recall that entitled persons are often not aware of these, being instead focused on their absolute right to pursue superior status), and you are encouraged to practice empathy for others.

Just as with humility, serenity, and gratitude, the readiness for forgiveness needs practice, and here again the *Lectio, Meditatio, Oratio,* and *Contemplatio* prayer experiences may enhance and complement the therapeutic guidelines outlined above. Using Scripture and the tradition of the Church , such as the lives of holy men and women, as material for *Lectio* prayer, you might learn new ways of exercising forgiveness in your own life. Through imagery and dialogue exercises with Jesus (*Meditatio*), and placing yourself in scenes where Jesus is insulted or misunderstood and He responds with empathy, you would express your own inclinations and allow yourself to hear His response. Ask for the grace to see things differently (*Oratio*), that your will might conform more to His than to your own sense of justice and fairness. And finally, practice acts of forgiveness, first by cultivating a heightened sense of His spirit working through you (*Contemplatio*) and then acting as a sign of His presence in the world, doing what He would do, even when you may at first think that you are going too far in extending forgiveness.

If you give yourself over to these exercises to counter the entitlement lifetrap, you may notice over time that you are less inclined to seek your own designs first, and in fact that you are less anxious, less hostile, more graced with a humble and serene acceptance of your privileged—but not superior—place in the world. Your addiction to control and the many other addictions that it drives will also likely dissipate, and you will experience a far greater pleasure than control—a life of freedom simply to live and let live.

# 6

# Will Anyone Ever Recognize MY Needs?

HAVE you often felt that your life is consumed with meeting the needs of others, and that nobody is really paying attention to your wishes or feelings? Perhaps you are engaged in a career that is service oriented, and you are very conscientious about taking care of others, but you secretly resent the lack of care for you. Do the demands of your family summon all of your attention, so that at the end of the day your own thoughts and feelings are left unexpressed? Why is this?

Maybe you are just too busy, and the remedy may simply entail scheduling some time for yourself to speak with a friend, your partner, or a family member. On the other hand, the problem may be more complicated than that. You may actually have the time and opportunity to express your own thoughts and feelings, but you may be reluctant to do so, fearing that you may lose the love and approval of those whose demands you are expected to gratify with your labors. It may be that your partner expects you to accomplish certain tasks around the house, but you want to focus your time and energy on other pursuits. Rather than openly discussing your feelings, however, you avoid expressing your dissatisfaction and focus instead on your partner's need for your help. Again and again, you surrender your own feelings and wishes to avoid offending others, and potentially—or likely, in your mind—losing their affection and approval. You are left with the overwhelming sense that it is impossible to get others to recognize your needs without risking anger, retaliation, or abandonment.

From a ST perspective, you may be unduly influenced by the *subjugation* lifetrap, which is an excessive focus on the desires, feelings, and responses of others, at the expense of your own needs, in order to gain love and approval, maintain a sense of connection, and avoid retaliation. Rate the following statements that are designed to measure this lifetrap, again taken from the Young Schema Questionnaire, by using the scoring key to determine how much you believe each of them is true of you.

### Scoring Key

1   Completely untrue of me
2   Mostly untrue of me
3   Slightly more true than untrue of me
4   Moderately true of me
5   Mostly true of me
6   Describes me perfectly

### Subjugation Questionnaire

____ 1. I often surrender control to other people in my life.

____ 2. I pay more attention to the needs and wishes of others than to what I am really feeling.

____ 3. I have let others unduly influence my life.

____ 4. I usually hold my opinions to myself.

____ 5. I spend too much time worrying about meeting others' wishes and demands.

____ 6. It's very difficult for me to disagree with others.

_____ 7. I do too much for others and not enough for myself.

_____ 8. I have a hard time asking others to take care of me.

_____ 9. I act as if I can get by on very little emotional support.

_____10. It's only right to put the needs of others ahead of mine.

**_____Your Total Score on Subjugation**
(Add your scores for statements 1-10)

### Interpreting Your Lifetrap Total Score

| | | |
|---|---|---|
| 10-19 | Very low | This lifetrap probably does not apply to you. |
| 20-29 | Fairly low | This lifetrap may only apply occasionally. |
| 30-39 | Moderate | This lifetrap is an issue in your life. |
| 40-49 | High | This is an important lifetrap for you. |
| 50-60 | Very high | This is one of your core lifetraps. |

If you labor under this lifetrap, you are likely to suffer from a host of personal and interpersonal difficulties, including problems with a secure self-identity, distrust of others' love, profound lonely feelings, and a build-up of rage frequently leading to impulsive and self-destructive behaviors.

If you are continually preoccupied with fulfilling obligations, especially those you'd rather not do, just to hold onto the relationships in your life, then you are not secure enough in your own value to others. A lifelong pattern of focusing on the opinions and desires of others at the expense of your own may have led you to become overly dependent on them for reassurance, guidance, and support, not because you believe that you are inherently incompetent (recall the *dependence* lifetrap), but because you are desperately afraid of losing your connection with them if you show any signs of dissent.

The *subjugation* lifetrap undermines your capacity to give and receive real love, because you fear that all love is conditional upon the successful completion of expectations that come from others, at the expense of your own needs and wishes. As a consequence, you probably doubt that anyone can sincerely accept and love you as you are, leading you to feel acutely alone in this world.

The excessive compliance associated with this position often generates a great deal of anger and resentment. Since you are too afraid to express that anger directly, it is more prone to surface in indirect ways, often leading to uncontrolled outbursts of anger, acting out behaviors (alcohol or drug abuse, reckless driving, sexual promiscuity), or in psychosomatic symptoms (headaches, backaches, muscle spasms).

Just as with the other lifetraps, subjugation has its origins in early childhood experiences with parents, siblings, and peers. Young claims that the family atmosphere for those who develop the subjugation lifetrap is one of conditional acceptance, whereby children are required to suppress their own feelings and needs to meet the emotional needs and desires of others. For example, if a parent is alcoholic and the child is used to monitoring the parent's mood to guide her requests for that day, rather than focusing on her own wishes, the child is likely to develop the subjugation lifetrap. In other cases, where the parents are frequently arguing and the child does everything to restore peace, often at his own expense, then that child, too, is likely to develop the subjugation lifetrap.

From a psychological perspective, the core problem for those influenced by the subjugation lifetrap is a profound sense of ambivalence about oneself and others. You are at once chomping at the bit to express your wants and needs to someone who will listen, and at the same time you are scared to death to do so, for fear of rejection and retaliation. Likewise, you want more than anything to believe that others can take time for you and respect your needs and wishes, but at the same time you believe that all love is conditional and people are ultimately only interested in you as long as you are meeting their needs. Marsha Linehan in her work with borderline personalities—people who often endorse this ambivalence about self and others that is associated with the subjugation lifetrap—has developed a treatment called Dialectical Behavior Therapy (DBT). This psychological treatment attempts to integrate sound therapeutic interventions with a spiritual (Zen) approach to change. Linehan has identified three core dialectical, or opposing tendencies that describe this ambivalence:

1. Intense Experience of Emotion versus Over-Control of Emotion

2. Passivity in Problem-Solving versus Apparent Competence

3. Unrelenting Crises versus Inhibited Grieving

First, because the subjugation lifetrap indicates that your emotions are not valid or welcome—that they threaten your connection with others—you may over-control your feelings by minimizing or denying them, or becoming self-accusatory or even self-punitive for having them (e.g., I shouldn't be resentful about taking care of my aging parents instead of relaxing after a long week at work). On the other end of the dialectic, you may over-react to them as the pressure of unexpressed affect builds up inside you with nowhere to go except out.

Secondly, as you have learned to focus exclusively on the needs and wishes of others in making decisions, you may be prone to passivity in problem-solving on matters that are purely personal (e.g., losing weight, joining a gym, recreating), and at the other end of the dialectic you may pretend that you are perfectly competent to handle life's challenges on your own.

Thirdly, because the anger that you feel has never found an appropriate and satisfying expression, you are likely to completely inhibit it and to avoid the issues that drive it, by means of avoidant and escapist behaviors (alcohol and substance abuse, impulsive behaviors), or on the other side of the dialectic to release the anger in its raw form, without reference to specific triggers as a global, undifferentiated response to internal pressure. This end of the dialectic may result in unrelenting crises, occasioned by diffuse anger whose origin and target is confused and unnamed.

In order to resolve this dialectic and arrive at a healthier balance between these extreme and opposite positions, changes in your ways of thinking, feeling, behaving, and relating to others are necessary. If you were in ST treatment, the therapist would challenge your ways of exaggerating the negative consequences of expressing your needs directly. Your ideas about how dangerous it is to express your feelings, needs, and wishes would be directly countered with more adaptive, less rigid thoughts (e.g., "Some people are capable of listening to my desires, even when they are contradictory to theirs, and will not retaliate or reject me for expressing them").

Linehan emphasizes the need for spiritual acceptance to accomplish this shift in your way of thinking. Spiritual acceptance is defined as the "developed capacity to fully embrace whatever is in the present moment." This includes all of your thoughts, feelings, and desires. It does not mean that you ought to put these impulses into action, at least not immediately, but that you should simply notice them. Give them some air time in your consciousness, precisely because they are part of your spirit in the present moment. After all, how can anyone else be expected to notice your needs, if you often ignore or dismiss them yourself? It is likely that this ready dismissal of your unwanted or dangerous thoughts is at the center of your emotional distress.

A key Zen principle is that emotional distress is often created because people cling to things as they wish they would be— or think they should be—instead of accepting things as they are. The practice of mindfulness, presented at more length in Chapter Three, is a spiritual tool that can be of great assistance in promoting the tolerance of all of your thoughts and feelings. Remember that it is important simply to notice your feelings and impulses, and to ride them out, without needing to do anything about them, at least not immediately.

Changing your own way of thinking about, or tolerating, your feelings and desires, by reducing the sense of danger associated with them, will also require that you engage in imaginary and actual experiences of expressing yourself more directly with others. In the context of ST, this process would likely involve the use of imagery, in which you express your anger and assert your wishes directly to the parent who first subjugated you as a child. The therapist would assist you in finding the words to identify the feelings that have been hidden and unexpressed. As an adult, you now have the resources and independence from your parents that will enable you to say these things with less fear of rejection or retaliation, and this expression in imagery is an important model for future interactions with significant others in your life.

Spiritual imagery is also an important tool for accomplishing more direct self-expression. Your sense of ambivalence about yourself and others that has resulted from your *subjugation* lifetrap has probably influenced your image of God. It would not be surprising for you to imagine God as loving you only conditionally, since He is unable or unwilling to accept all of your wishes and feelings, especially your anger. This expectation is likely to contribute to your sense of anger and resentment toward God.

Through *Meditatio* prayer, you can take a scene from Scripture—perhaps one of the prophets directly expressing anger at God for some situation of injustice—and imagine yourself in that scene expressing to God your anger about feeling neglected, undervalued, and disrespected. Try not to rush to concluding the prayer by offering God or yourself an easy resolution. Simply stay with the anger, and give God the time to hear you out. Steady and repeated practices of this sort are likely to contribute to your own sense of the value of your feelings and of the acceptability of their expression.

Over time, your ambivalence about yourself and others may have also undermined your sense of God's constancy. As with other interpersonal relationships, when you are feeling good, then you see God as kind, loving, and responsive to your feelings, but when you are feeling angry or depressed, then you are likely to see God as distant or rejecting. It is as if your image of God is dependent on your mood. *Contemplatio* prayer, simply noticing God as faithful and present ("Be still and know that I am God"), especially when you are feeling angry or despondent, may successfully challenge your lifetrap expectations that others' love is conditional.

Finally, the work of converting your ambivalence into a more accepting stance toward yourself and others requires actual experiences of directly expressing your feelings, especially the negative ones, to others whom you can trust. While the therapy relationship is ideally a safe place to start asserting yourself, you may find this kind of validating environment in the context of spiritual direction, through participation in support groups, or through more informal interactions with individuals who are knowledgeable about your lifetrap and are committed to fostering your expression of feelings without retaliating or rejecting you. These supportive others would ideally encourage you to make more choices without requiring their explicit approval, thereby fostering your active problem-solving without fear of rejection. It is important for you to choose these people carefully, because your lifetrap may influence you (recall the process of lifetrap maintenance explained in Chapter 1) to select those who will only reinforce your fears and expectations. With the right persons, you can practice again and again the direct expression of your feelings, and learn to validate them and to expect the same from others. The anger and resentment that have built up over the years will gradually dissipate, and your experience of yourself, others, and God will become a more reliable source of understanding and acceptance.

# 7

# I Can't Slow Down

❧

DO you have a hard time taking time off, relaxing, playing, letting go of your duties and responsibilities long enough to find some refreshment and peace of mind? Do you frequently worry that your performance may not be up to certain standards, so that you impose strict limits on yourself to get things accomplished, often to the exclusion of relaxation and sometimes at the expense of satisfying interpersonal relationships? You may find that despite your high standards and a great deal of time invested in accomplishing tasks at work and at home that you are still not satisfied with your performance. You may even want to change this approach to your life but simply can't, for fear of criticism or of falling completely out of control.

If these behaviors and beliefs sound like you, you may be compulsively attached to control. While orderliness and high standards are desirable traits that are often associated with success at work, an excessive preoccupation with control makes you particularly prone to workaholism. The danger with this approach to work is that, despite considerable success at your performance, you are likely to experience emotional turmoil, often anxiety and depression, along with a host of physical maladies associated with high stress. Also, if your workaholic tendencies are accompanied by an obsessional, perfectionistic attention to detail, you are likely to alienate your co-workers. The work product also suffers under these conditions, as your micromanagement style may ignore the larger picture and impede the development of a more expedient plan of action.

Perhaps even more toxic than impaired work performance is the likelihood of unsatisfying personal relationships. You may find that you are unable to relax these standards and rules, especially when it would be appropriate to do so. You are always organizing, making lists, following rules from which you refuse to deviate, even temporarily. When you go away on vacation, you carry this same approach to the planning and living of this "free" time, frequently sapping the joy out of this time for yourself and your loved ones. It's not that you intend this outcome—thus the compulsive nature of this approach to life—but that you are afraid to try something different. You can't slow down.

From a ST perspective, you may be laboring under the influence of the *unrelenting standards* lifetrap. Rate the following statements that are designed to measure this lifetrap, again taken from the Young Schema Questionnaire, by using the scoring key to determine how much you believe each of them is true of you.

### Scoring Key

1  Completely untrue of me
2  Mostly untrue of me
3  Slightly more true than untrue of me
4  Moderately true of me
5  Mostly true of me
6  Describes me perfectly

### Unrelenting Standards Questionnaire

_____ 1. I have to be number one at everything that I do, or else I get very angry and frustrated.

_____ 2. I am never satisfied with my accomplishments.

_____ 3. I will never settle for anything less than perfection.

_____ 4. I must always be ready to meet challenges successfully.

_____ 5. I will always sacrifice play time to get something
important done.

_____ 6. My family and friends are frequently upset with me
because I don't spend enough quality time with them.

_____ 7. I feel the pressure of my responsibilities sometimes in
my body, e.g., headaches, backaches, stomachaches.

_____ 8. I believe that any mistake could possibly lead to very
serious consequences.

_____ 9. I am always striving to get ahead of others.

_____10. I am very concerned about securing my financial and
professional status.

_____**Your Total Score on Unrelenting Standards**
(Add scores for statements 1-10)

### Interpreting Your Lifetrap Total Score

| | | |
|---|---|---|
| 10-19 | Very low | This lifetrap probably does not apply to you. |
| 20-29 | Fairly low | This lifetrap may only apply occasionally. |
| 30-39 | Moderate | This lifetrap is an issue in your life. |
| 40-49 | High | This is an important lifetrap for you. |
| 50-60 | Very high | This is one of your core lifetraps. |

Young describes this lifetrap as the belief that you must
strive to meet very high, internalized standards of behavior
and performance, usually to avoid criticism. This lifetrap

results in (1) feelings of pressure or difficulty slowing down (e.g., having a hard time taking a day off from work); (2) a hypercritical attitude toward yourself and others; and (3) the presence of lots of "shoulds" in your life.

The typical family of origin for this lifetrap is demanding and sometimes punitive, placing emphasis on performance, duty, and perfectionism over pleasure, joy, and relaxation. You may have come from a family that was overly concerned with achievement, high grades, and recognition for accomplishments, at the expense of play and spontaneity. If so, you may have a hard time even now validating your accomplishments or drawing satisfaction from them. You may be more likely to focus on the faults and flaws in your work and to be anxious and pressured to perform better. You can rarely say to yourself or others, "I'm happy with what I have done. Now, it's time to relax and celebrate the completion of the task."

Psychologically, the healing of this lifetrap entails a radical change in the way you think about life and your relationship to your work. You will have to identify your priorities in order to achieve a balance between work and play, accomplishment and rest, success and simply being. In ST, you would be encouraged to make a list of your high standards—as a worker, parent, spouse, friend—and to weigh their advantages and disadvantages in terms of your health and happiness, as well as your performance. You are likely to discover that your unrealistically high standards may account for your success in one area, but be detrimental to your performance in another. In therapy, you would also be challenged to list all of the risks that you associate with slowing down, such as being open to criticism, failure, loss of control, and then to generate alternate reasonable outcomes, e.g., others may understand and support your need for rest and relaxation, or you may feel an even greater sense of control over your time. In Twelve-Step programs, slogans like "Progress, not perfection" are often very helpful to counter this compulsive preoccupation with performance.

Your image of God may need to change, too, in order to accommodate a healthier perspective on your life and labor. You may be used to seeing God as a parental taskmaster or police officer,watching you and waiting to criticize or punish you if you slow down or make a mistake. Sperry points out that certain Scriptures, such as,"Be perfect, as your heavenly Father is perfect" reinforce this expectation. While this exhortation is intended to counter complacency and to channel our energies to the promotion of the heavenly realm, it is not intended to pressure us into the unrelenting pursuit of perfection, at the expense of enjoying the gift of life, as imperfect and unfinished as it is given to us.

More helpful images of God to counter your unrelenting standards lifetrap are in creation accounts of God's taking delight in humanity, or of Jesus's embracing children or eating with His disciples. These images highlight the playful, spontaneous side of God. Jesus certainly recognized the importance and urgency of His mission, but this acknowledgement did not impede Him from taking time to rest, pray, and recreate with His friends. You may profitably spend time praying with images of God as attentive to your true needs (Lk 12:22-31), freeing you to release your anxiety about controlling your life and allowing you to focus instead on the more important things in life. *Meditatio* prayer experiences with these images may help to promote your own acceptance of the need for play and spontaneity in your life.

Changes in your prayer style, too, may help you to slow down. Your unrelenting standards lifetrap may have influenced you to focus your prayer on your own faults, failings, and short-comings, rather than on the loving and steady presence of God who simply wants to be with you as you are in the moment. Sperry points out that obsessive-compulsive personalities will hear and say the words: "Lord, I am not worthy that you should come under my roof, but speak the words and I shall be healed," but they can only allow themselves to believe the first part, "Lord, I am not worthy," and find it almost impossible to believe that they can be healed and be worthy. Perhaps a more helpful passage to pray with is: "You are my beloved in whom I am well pleased." Simply using that passage, in a *Contemplatio* prayer, recognizing that you are loved as you are, without having to come up with any new ideas, projects, or initiatives, is a useful remedy for the compulsive tendency to perform. You can simply waste time with the Lord. At the same time, you will be cultivating self-acceptance, by empathizing with God and His love for you instead of your feelings of shame that have been fostered by your perfectionism.

As with all lifetraps, your unrelenting standards have likely fostered an unacknowledged and unspoken anger and resentment at your parents who first established and enforced them for you. In ST, this anger would be expressed through imagery and dialogues with your parents; you would tell them about your disappointment at having to sacrifice your realistic and healthy need for play and spontaneity in order to meet their unrealistically high standards of performance.

In your prayer, as well, you might address this disappointment to God in an imaginary exercise or through a dialogue. You would tell God about your fear of His criticism and how you followed all the rules, commandments, and precepts of your faith out of duty more than as a response of love. Allow God to tell you that you are beloved, not because you follow the rules so well, but simply because you are His creature: "You are my beloved, in whom I am well pleased." Let God convince you that it is okay to slow down.

Whether in therapy or through another form of structured change, you will want to translate your new way of thinking about yourself and your standards of performance into behavioral changes. Gradually, you may want to increase your playtime and to give yourself permission to stop work at a certain hour, or after so many hours dedicated to a given project, even if you are not yet finished with it. In your prayer, too, you might agree to spend time regularly playing with God, not taking yourself or your time with God so seriously. You might simply take a walk with God, or eat with Him, or enjoy a sunrise in the presence of the Holy One, without needing to finish your list of petitions or read another spiritual book. You might pray for the grace to see time as a gift, and not as an enemy, so that you will welcome it, and not fear its passage or try to control or "beat time."

Perhaps the greatest spiritual antidote to the anxiety associated with the *unrelenting standards* lifetrap is the cultivation of serenity. Serenity has been defined variously as peace of mind or inner peace. "Lamb of God, who takes away the sin of the world, grant us peace," we pray just before Holy Communion. Peace or serenity is not just something to hope for on a sunny day; it is as essential as bread to our life and well-being, and it is all the more necessary for you who struggle against slowing down. Maslow emphasized the need to bring calmness into one's psychological state, and he asserted that we need the serene as well as the poignantly emotional. Serenity has been popularized in our culture by the Twelve-Step Program ("God grant me the serenity to accept the things I cannot change"), and it includes acceptance of life on life's terms, trust in God's will, and having a present day orientation, as opposed to dwelling on past guilt or future anxiety. As such, serenity can replace chronic anxiety with joy. But how do you attain this serenity?

Roberts and Cunningham highlight the importance of detachment as the vehicle for attaining serenity. Whereas your attachment to predict and control your performance is holding you back from slowing down enough to enjoy your life, detachment entails giving yourself some emotional space in between the impulse to perform and the act of performing. Detachment involves letting go of the fear of criticism, loss of control, or failure. In his book on the lifetraps that sabotage happiness, *The Myth of More*, Joseph Novello, MD, underscores this notion: "Attachment is built on fear, the fear that we will not obtain this or that, or—once we do—that we will lose it. It demands that we remain focused on the deficits in our lives . . . The detached person, on the other hand, remains focused on the surplus in his life. Attachment breeds anxiety. Detachment begets serenity."

There are several simple methods that you can employ to enhance this healthy sense of detachment and to assist you in slowing down. Start with your breathing. Take some time each day simply to notice your own breath, coming into your mouth cool and going out your nose warm. Or, you may want to let your hand rest gently on your abdomen, and simply notice how it expands as you inhale and contracts as you exhale. As you focus on your breathing, quietly observe all of your thoughts and feelings, especially the anxious ones, and simply let them pass through your awareness. As you cultivate these methods of passive awareness with time and practice, you will notice that you will become more comfortable with slowing down.

Mindfulness meditation can also be a useful spiritual tool in healing from the unrelenting standards lifetrap. By bringing your complete attention to the present experience, and thereby ignoring or dismissing your obsessive preoccupations with work or achievement, you can cultivate an attitude of acceptance of all the thoughts, emotions, and events of your life, without trying to correct or immediately change them. Sometimes, when the intrusions of things to be done or problems to be solved get in the way of practicing mindfulness, it is useful to make an agreement with yourself that you will set aside a period of time (usually 20-30 minutes) later in the day when you will do nothing but focus on these issues. Then, you will be free to concentrate on the present, and this reorientation of your attention will likely diffuse the negativity, anger, and hostility that can be associated with feeling pressured to resolve all the issues in your life. As pointed out in Chapter 3, the practice of mindfulness has been associated with a host of benefits to physical, emotional, and spiritual well-being, including relaxation, increased concentration, positive feelings toward oneself and others, and a heightened sense of harmony with God.

Finding an inner haven in the midst of the frenzy of your life is an essential step in successfully overcoming this lifetrap. Try to imagine a safe place where you would feel completely relaxed—it can be an imaginary or real place, in your present or past—and use that image to assist you in breathing or mindfulness meditation exercises. People with the unrelenting standards lifetrap often have a difficult time even imagining such a place, so you may ask someone whom you trust to give you some ideas. These images may be sparked by or cultivated with a visual scene, a familiar song, taste, or smell. Engaging your senses may distract you from your thoughts and preoccupations long enough to begin the prayer exercises outlined above. St. Ignatius in his *Spiritual Exercises* advises the retreatant to apply all five senses to a particular passage from Scripture to assist in entering the scene more completely, with full mind and heart.

Jack Kornfield, in his book *A Path with Heart*, describes some key characteristics of spiritual maturity, including openness, integrity, and ordinariness, and these qualities may serve as guideposts against which to measure your success at overcoming your unrelenting standards. Openness to change, to becoming something more than you can imagine or predict, runs counter to the unrelenting standards lifetrap, by shifting your focus from a disproportionate need to control the direction of your life, and toward a greater acceptance that you are a work-in-progress. While it is probably true that this trait of openness is more natural to some than others, it can be fostered through seeking God in nature, plays, novels, music, and with new people. It entails a willingness to be surprised by God.

Integrity is not perfection, although your unrelenting standards may confuse these ideals and motivate you to cultivate secret compartments of thoughts, feelings, and behaviors that you believe to be less than, or even opposite to, what you "should" be thinking and feeling. These secrets get in the way of your slowing down, as you are likely driven to compensate for them through your achievements at home or at work. Spiritual maturity, as characterized by integrity, involves sharing your secrets—faults, flaws, liabilities—with a trusted person, whether your therapist, spiritual director, or personal friend, without fear of criticism or rejection.

Finally, and of course related to openness and integrity, a sense of ordinariness is a mark of success at overcoming your unrelenting standards lifetrap. Robert Wicks, in *Touching the Holy*, points out that nowhere in the Bible is there a single instance of Christ clinging to His divinity. Wicks observes: "He was not as obsessed with His image as we so often are with ours." By becoming less critical of yourself and others and by accepting that what you need, after all, is not success at all you do but love for who you are, you are able to slow down and live the life you have been given more abundantly.

# Part III

# Choosing the Right Kind of Support

IT must be clear to you by now that lifetraps are rigid, inflexible beliefs that often require a great deal of energy and persistence to confront and change on your own. For some people, identifying and changing them will require considerable assistance, including professional intervention, while for others this process may be accomplished with the help of a friend or some trusted companion. One criterion to guide your decision about whether to seek help is the extent to which your lifetraps may be causing anxiety, depression, anger, hostility, and other negative emotions in your life. Another criterion is the degree of impairment in your interpersonal relationships. For example, if your problems with others at home or at work are related to one of your lifetraps and are serious enough to challenge the stability of those relationships, then you would be well advised to seek outside support in identifying and implementing strategies to weaken those lifetraps. On the other hand, if your emotional and relational life is satisfactory, but perhaps in need of fine-tuning to become even more gratifying and productive, then you might consider reflecting upon the lifetrap beliefs outlined in this text and using some of the psychological and spiritual tools presented here on your own or with a close, personal friend.

As described in Chapter 1, Schema Therapy (ST) is a systematic psychotherapy approach designed specifically to identify and change lifetrap beliefs and their effects on your thinking, feeling, behaving, and relating to others. As a psychological intervention, it does not directly incorporate the spiritual perspective or spiritual resources described in this book, but it is certainly conceivable that someone might engage in ST, and at the same time use some of these spiritual tools as adjuncts to the therapy process. The next chapter will present specific criteria for making this choice for therapy, along with some practical suggestions for how to proceed.

Another possibility for implementing a psycho-spiritual approach would be to work with a spiritual director, either as the principal modality for change or along with formal counseling. In this case, the spiritual director would need to be knowledgeable enough about lifetraps—specifically about whether to refer you at some point to therapy— to complement the work accomplished in direction. Chapter 9 will present the advantages of spiritual direction, qualities to look for in a spiritual director, and again some practical ways to find one.

Finally, if you believe that your lifetraps are mild and that your life might improve by reading more about them and making some spiritual changes in your life, Chapter 10 will present guidelines for cultivating a practice of spiritual reading along with some suggestions to enhance your spiritual growth.

# 8

# Seeking Professional Counseling

HOW do you know if you need professional counseling for your lifetraps? One of the key criterion is the nature and severity of the problems that are brought about by them. For example, if your lifetrap (e.g., *emotional deprivation*) results in bouts of serious depression—not just in feeling blue occasionally or having a bad day from time to time, but in having sustained periods of time, usually at least two weeks, of sad or irritable mood, hopelessness or guilt, loss of pleasure in the activities that were usually enjoyable, changes in appetite or sleep, and especially the presence of thoughts of suicide—then you would be well advised to seek professional help. Or perhaps your lifetrap has led to pathological levels of anxiety (*unrelenting standards*), so that you are constantly worrying, or you develop social and performance anxieties, or an obsessive-compulsive disorder (i.e., unwanted, intrusive thoughts which heighten anxiety and are followed by compulsive rituals to weaken the anxiety). In some cases, lifetraps (*abandonment, mistrust/abuse*) are signals of earlier trauma (e.g., physical or sexual abuse, emotional neglect), and as such may result in nightmares, flashbacks, emotional outbursts, and many more symptoms associated with exposure to trauma. Lifetraps (*entitlement*) may also be risk factors for substance abuse and other addictions, as discussed in Chapter 5.

If any of these serious problems are yours, then you might first seek confirmation from a trusted friend or family member to verify your perception of the problem and its severity. Alternatively, you may want to go directly to a helping professional for testing or for a clinical opinion about the nature and severity of your problem. If you are specifically interested in identifying and changing the lifetraps that are driving your emotional, behavioral, or relational problems, then you would do well to consult a ST trained therapist, as not all therapists are knowledgeable about lifetrap theory and strategies to change them.

## Choosing a Mental Health Professional

Generally speaking, there are three kinds of mental health professionals who practice within the disciplines of psychology, social work, or psychiatry. Psychologists are uniquely and extensively trained at the doctoral level in formal assessment instruments and techniques, as well as the practice of psychotherapy. Clinical social workers are trained at the master's level in psychotherapy and they often provide services at lower cost than psychologists. Psychiatrists are medical doctors, and to date they are the only mental health professionals who prescribe medications; their services are often necessary for people whose mental health is too seriously compromised to benefit from psychotherapy alone

While there is certainly diversity among mental health professionals with respect to areas of practice and specialization, two key considerations ought to inform your choice. First, what is the background and training of this provider? What kinds of clients has she treated—children, adolescents, adults, families? What problem areas has she successfully treated—depression, substance abuse, marriage problems? What is her theoretical orientation? Some clinicians are strictly behavioral and symptom focused, and they would likely miss or ignore the relevance of lifetraps to your present problems. Others are trained to focus either on infantile conflicts or only on current thoughts and beliefs, without integrating them in the way presented by Young in Schema Therapy. These clinicians would also miss or ignore the presence and function of lifetraps in your life.

Secondly, you would do well to schedule an initial interview with a prospective therapist, to determine how comfortable you are with this person, and to inquire about whether she is respectful of your religious beliefs and willing to work with them in the context of psychotherapy. Often, you will get a sense of whether or not the therapist is comfortable—or at least non-judgmental about—your spiritual beliefs and religious practices, in the very first meeting.

Once you determine that the therapist is knowledgeable about lifetraps and supportive of your relationship with God, then you are ready to determine the parameters of treatment. More specifically, you will want answers to the following questions: What is the cost, and is there a sliding scale? Is there a policy of charging you for missed sessions?

In order to determine the frequency—weekly, bi-weekly, monthly—and duration—six months, twelve months, or longer—of your treatment, you will probably need to provide the therapist with a description of your problem. If you are seeing a ST therapist, this process will be facilitated by the therapist, who will use specific techniques—life history review, schema questionnaires like the ones in this text, and imagery exercises—to elicit information and to guide the treatment. Your own expectations for therapy are also an important ingredient in deciding the course of your treatment. Your commitment to coming to each of the scheduled sessions and doing the homework that is frequently assigned in ST will likely accelerate your progress.

## Adding a Spiritual Dimension to Your Treatment

As described at length in Chapter 2, prayer exercises and other spiritual resources may profitably complement the change strategies of ST. Praying with passages from Scripture, using imagery and prayer dialogues to work through fears of rejection, anger at perceived helplessness, or any of the other negative emotions associated with lifetraps, can be a very useful way to strengthen the changes made through therapy. Some contend that for certain problems, therapy is not effective without integrating this spiritual dimension in treatment. For example, if you have experienced the loss of a loved one through death or permanent and irreversible separation, you may attempt to mourn that loss through psychological techniques, but the abiding source of consolation that comes from believing that that person is in heaven or dwelling with God is arguably the necessary condition for successfully completing that mourning process. Only when you are reassured by faith and a connection with a God who transcends death can you allow yourself to deliver your loved one into the hands of that eternal source of love. Prayer images and dialogues with God, in which you actively commit your loved one to God, can open the door for your acceptance of the loss and for reinvesting your energy in this life. Otherwise, the lifetraps that are potentially triggered by such a loss—*abandonment, emotional deprivation, mistrust*—are only reinforced, and their resolution is compromised by the painful fact that people do indeed leave forever.

As a complement to your work in therapy, you may be inclined to pursue the spiritual dimension of your recovery from lifetraps on your own, in the context of personal prayer and through some of the techniques described in this book. On the other hand, it may be useful to pray through a particular lifetrap with a friend or partner with whom you can share your journey and perhaps participate in their own process as well. Sometimes, spiritual recovery is assisted greatly through group participation, as in the case of groups organized around issues of bereavement, depression, substance abuse, or social anxiety. Irvin Yalom writes in his classic text, *The Theory and Practice of Group Psychotherapy*, that through group participation and interpersonal feedback, you are likely to reduce your sense of alienation—of feeling isolated with your lifetrap—and to increase your sense of hope, by interacting with others who are also struggling to overcome their lifetraps and the problems associated with them. Beyond these gains that are associated with group therapy in general, the added dimension of a spiritual perspective in this group context can strengthen your own faith and promote your healing and growth. You will likely find help not only to endure your pain and to discover useful ways to change lifetrap beliefs, but also to derive meaning from your pain, in the context of God's will for your life.

Participation in a spiritual support group is therefore a worthy consideration. At the same time, starting such a group in your own parish or local community will require some initiative and organizational skill. For example, if you were to begin a group to address the needs of people who are experiencing a recent loss and some of the attendant feelings of anxiety, depression, and perhaps the *abandonment* lifetrap belief that no one will ever again be available for connection and support, then you would want to make sure that the candidates for membership in this group would commit to participating weekly for a given period of time, usually three to six months. Regular attendance is important to the life of any group, but especially to one that is committed to restoring a faith in dependability following a significant loss. One person in the group will function as the coordinator, and that person will be in charge of scheduling and convening meetings. People would each commit to confidentiality within the group—not sharing what happens there with anyone else, including their respective family members. Each member would take responsibility for leading the group by selecting a Scripture passage to begin, facilitating the discussion, keeping track of the time and closing the meeting on time.

Ordinarily, it is a good idea to select a topic for each meeting, e.g., recognizing your *abandonment* lifetrap, although occasionally it may be useful to dedicate a meeting to an open discussion forum. You will also want to set aside some time for group prayer—to listen to the Word of God as it informs and consoles the group members. You may want to invite a mental health professional into the group early in your meetings to give more specific guidelines on the boundaries and possibilities for your group and its goals. The leader of the group would probably want to spend some time speaking with a mental health professional prior to convening the group, to establish realistic goals and procedures. Admittedly, this preparation may be time-consuming, but the benefits to the participants are well worth the efforts.

# 9

# Spiritual Direction

WHETHER you choose to address and change your life-traps through ST or not, one spiritual resource that you may consider is spiritual direction. Unlike the ST therapist, the spiritual director is explicitly committed to facilitating your experience of God and to promoting your faith life. In fact, William Barry and William Connolly argue that the director must be of the same faith community as the directee, precisely to be able to speak knowledgeably about the experience of God in a particular context, whether Christian, Jewish, or other. A spiritual director, according to Barry and Connolly, will optimally en-able you to pay closer attention to God's personal communication with you, to grow in intimacy with God, and to live out the consequences of that relationship.

Francis Houdek, S.J. defines spiritual direction as "a conversation—a dialogue—between two people, where one person aids another to express his or her experience of personal faith and personal mystery." It is important to note that the purpose of the conversation between the spiritual director and directee is always to foster a more intimate conversation between the directee and God. This focus, of course, is another point of distinction between therapy and spiritual direction, as the former is interested in promoting conversation with a host of persons from your past (parents, siblings) and present (family, colleagues at work, etc.) as a means of identifying and changing your lifetraps.

While both ST and spiritual direction aim to assist you in clarifying your own experience and in working through problematic issues to arrive at a more joyful and productive life, spiritual direction is explicitly aimed at integrating your present conflicts in the context of your faith experience. For example, if your *mistrust/abuse* lifetrap has been triggered by a recent break up of a romantic relationship, the likely intervention of the spiritual director will be to challenge you to identify the fears that no one is trustworthy and that you will never find an honest and reliable partner to stay with you, and then to wait for God to say something new to you about yourself and His plan for your life. Rather than acting out the anger associated with those fears, either by turning it against yourself by overeating, substance abuse, isolation, or on others by lying, cheating and manipulating them, the spiritual director would advocate taking the fear and the anger to prayer, dialoguing with God about your feelings, and giving God the time and opportunity to respond to you. Getting this response would, of course, require that you pay attention, through the various spiritual means outlined in this text and others that may be suggested to you by the director. It would be the task of that director, then, to confirm or disconfirm God's response to you, not through some special magical connection that he may have with God, but by discerning with you the divine will, in the context of your personal faith story. For this reason, it is important that the spiritual director accompany you not just through times of crisis, but through your ordinary lived faith experience, so that he may assist you in noticing God's characteristic presence in your life, especially during those times when it feels that God is absent.

In order to become aware of God's characteristic ways of relating to you, and to make the experience of spiritual direction a useful tool in your recovery from lifetraps, you will need to do your homework. Just as in ST, where you are given assignments to complete between sessions to monitor your thoughts, feelings, and behaviors, so too in spiritual direction you are expected to engage in regular spiritual practices so that your sessions are not reduced to chatting about current events in your life.

The daily practice of prayer is an essential component of effective spiritual direction. Paying attention to God through the various prayer forms described in this text is the best way to become familiar with Divine Providence working in your life. Keeping a journal can also assist this process. You would write for a few minutes after each prayer period about something that you noticed in the prayer material, about any new insights, or about how you were feeling during that time of prayer. Taking time each day—perhaps ten or fifteen minutes at the end of the day—simply to ask yourself, "Where was God today?" or "What am I grateful for today?" can also help you to stay tuned in to God's presence and activity in your life.

## Qualities to Seek in a Spiritual Director

A satisfying and productive experience of spiritual direction also depends on certain qualities of the director. First of all, as the process requires conversation and the mutual sharing of faith, you will need someone who can easily engage in dialogue. It is not helpful for the director to maintain the role of advice-giver, or to relate to you as expert to learner, since these relational patterns often distract the focus from you and your experience. Sometimes the director will be silent to allow you to have a voice, and to hear in that voice the promptings of the Spirit leading you to growth in truth and holiness.

A second essential characteristic of the spiritual director is the capacity for empathy. This does not mean that directors must have actually experienced God in their lives in exactly the same way that you are, but that they are capable of understanding your experience from your perspective. This non-judgmental approach to you and your faith story is a necessary condition for the trust and honesty that will enable you to present your life issues—the good and the bad, the beautiful and the ugly—without fear or hesitation.

As the foundation for this relationship is the sharing of faith, you will need someone whose own faith is mature and continually growing. This will be evidenced by a transparent familiarity with Scripture and Church traditions, balanced with a strong pastoral sense and skill at applying the accumulated wisdom of the great spiritual writers and mystics to your particular life issues.

Besides knowledge of the faith, you will also benefit from a director who has a solid familiarity with human development, including the ordinary and extraordinary joys and sorrows of life, and some of the ways to intervene in times of suffering to promote healing and growth. If you are working to weaken your lifetraps and thereby to arrive at a new freedom and wholeness in your life, the director should have some knowledge of lifetrap origins and their effects on your mood, behavior, and relationships with God and others.

Moreover, the director should be honest enough to admit when he is working outside his competence, and to refer you to a mental health specialist when the problems are beyond the scope of spiritual direction. For example, if you are seriously depressed or in the throes of addiction, or if your relationships are too conflicted to understand and resolve with prayer and spiritual discernment, then the spiritual director would do well to discuss the limitations of spiritual direction alone and to facilitate your involvement in a psychotherapy like ST. Therapy in this case would not replace spiritual direction, but it would broaden the scope of intervention and accelerate progress to alleviate the chronic pain that fails to subside without it.

Above all, you will want a director who is capable of loving you, of seeing you as Christ sees you and confirming how God is inviting you to confront your lifetrap fears and anxieties in order to discover a new freedom in your life.

## Beginning Spiritual Direction

In order to identify a potential spiritual director, you will want to talk to some trusted friends who are in spiritual direction or you might call your local parish priest or a retreat or renewal center to recommend directors. Like choosing a therapist, it is important to interview prospective directors, and to discuss with them your expectations, as well as your commitment to the process in terms of time (usually spiritual direction takes place on a monthly basis) and money (some directors charge, others suggest a donation, and still others offer their services without charge). Ask the spiritual director to discuss her understanding of spiritual direction, as well as her experience, both in terms of gratifying and frustrating aspects. Once you select a director, suggest that you have regular evaluations of the direction—perhaps after the first three months, then every six months—to discuss whether your mutual expectations are being satisfied. It is always better to establish this arrangement before the direction begins, so that neither party feels unnecessarily criticized when the idea surfaces later in the working relationship.

At the first spiritual direction session, there are several possibilities for places to start. You might begin by relating your personal history, especially highlighting the place of God throughout your childhood, adolescence, and adult years. Alternatively, you might begin by presenting what is currently distressing you. If you have been in ST or are familiar with your lifetraps, you may want to present this to your new spiritual director as a context for understanding your current distress. If you are already praying, you might begin by noticing what is happening in your prayer—particular joys and consolations, or periods of dryness and desolation. Perhaps you are aware of religious conversion points in your life or you experience your prayer life as a roller coaster with periods of intense prayer followed by equally long periods of no prayer at all. Any of these observations would be appropriate starting points for spiritual direction.

Wherever you begin, it is reasonable to expect that spiritual direction will assist you in overcoming lifetraps, by heightening your awareness of God's action in the present. This will help not only to quell your fears and anxieties but to deepen your sense of meaning and value, so that you can more freely pursue the love and happiness you deserve as a child of God.

# 10

# Spiritual Reading

WHETHER you choose to work on your lifetraps in the context of therapy, spiritual direction, or through some other medium, spiritual reading can inform your reflections and focus your efforts at changing your unhealthy patterns of thinking, feeling, and relating to others. Unlike other types of reading, whether professional or recreational, spiritual reading is an exercise of prayer, and it requires a certain discipline to prepare for and to engage in this exercise profitably. There are guidelines to practice this discipline, and these cover the selection of reading material, the cultivation of a certain attitude during this time of reading, and the maintenance of supplementary practices to support and sustain the benefits of this exercise.

## Choosing the Texts

Among the many texts that you may choose for spiritual reading, the premier source remains the Bible, which is arguably the single most significant self-help book in human history. You may want to select a particular Gospel and read it , not with an eye toward exegesis or critical reading but as accounts of salvation that speak directly to your lifetrap recovery. For example, if you are aiming to challenge your abandonment lifetrap, you may read through the Gospel of Luke, showing Jesus loving His disciples. These accounts will support and strengthen the counter-belief to your lifetrap—that you will not be abandoned, emotionally deprived, or rejected by Jesus. Other sources in the Bible include the Psalms, the prayer book of the Church, in which human experiences of joy and hope, as well as desolation and despair, can serve to validate your life experiences and remind you that your lifetraps are not original or necessarily unique, but they are part of the human story and God has heard these pleas of desperation before, responding with mercy and love.

In addition to the sacred Scriptures, there is a vast body of literature on spirituality, prayer, and the life of faith that is recorded in primary and secondary sources. Writings of the Church Fathers and saints through the centuries—Athanasius, Gregory of Nyssa, Augustine, Bernard of Clairvaux, Teresa of Avila—are rich sources that testify to the power of faith, and they can be easily applied to your efforts at lifetrap recovery.

Poetry, drama, and other noted discourses can also be used for spiritual reading. One example might be a text written by Teilhard de Chardin, *The Divine Milieu*, in which you can profitably reflect on a passage such as the following:

> *The greater man becomes, the more humanity becomes united, with consciousness of, and mastery of, its potentialities, the more beautiful creation will be, the more perfect adoration will become, and the more Christ will find, for mystical extensions, a body worthy of resurrection. The world can no more have two summits than a circumference can have two centers. The star for which the world is waiting, without yet being able to give it a name, or rightly appreciate its true transcendence, or even recognize the most spiritual and divine of its rays, is, necessarily, Christ himself, in whom we hope.*

This is obviously not a text to be read swiftly, as if to gather some new information, but rather as a reflection that can be read and re-read to move you to prayer. It may provide a novel, decidedly mystical, context within which to consider your life-trap recovery.

Other sources for spiritual reading can be found online, where certain organizations post daily or weekly texts for prayerful reading and reflection. There are also numerous meditation books that highlight a different text for each day that can be used as prayer starters. Alternatively, you can select your texts according to certain themes that you are interested in pursuing, guided perhaps by your lifetrap recovery issues.

## Cultivating a Unique Attitude

Most of us are used to reading for information, whether for personal or professional purposes. You search keywords online, or you go to the library and search texts by call numbers. If you're lucky, you may even find a librarian willing to assist you in selecting relevant material.

This informational reading process is radically different from spiritual reading. The goal of spiritual reading, after all, is not to find some new information, but to enjoy the phrases, the wording, and the imagery, all designed to express the central tenets of our faith in a fresh and captivating way. You defeat your purpose if you rush through the text, instead of dwelling slowly and respectfully with the truth that is presented in it. St. Ignatius Loyola cautioned the reader of spiritual texts that it is not the amount of material covered which finally satisfies the soul, but deeply relishing the truth expressed therein. Alternatively stated, it is better to dig deeply to find water than to make many shallow holes.

Besides slowing down to appreciate spiritual reading, you would do well to cultivate an attitude of docility to approach these texts prayerfully. You may have been educated or trained to study texts critically—to compare them to other similar texts, to find flaws in arguments presented, grammar and phraseology, or to generate counter-arguments. As spiritual readers, this approach is a distraction from the reading as a form of prayer. Instead, you will want to welcome the text as a gift of the Holy Spirit to you for the unique circumstances of your life. The sacred Scriptures or the writings of the saints may not use the language of lifetraps, but the invitation to freedom from slavery—a common theme throughout these writings—is likely to speak directly to your lifetrap recovery issues. St. Francis de Sales, in his *Rule of Holy Living* (1649), advises the spiritual reader to "Look on what you read as though it were a letter addressed to you personally from the saints in heaven to guide you and encourage you on your way there."

## Fostering the Discipline of Spiritual Reading

As with other forms of prayer, spiritual reading requires a certain discipline. It is important to set aside a regular time for reading, perhaps fifteen minutes each day or an hour each week, when you have the energy to stay focused on the text. For this reason, it may not be a good idea to do spiritual reading at bedtime. You will want to read in a quiet, private place, where you are not likely to get interrupted and in a place that evokes your sense of being in the presence of the Holy One.

Choosing the text and reading it before the actual prayer time is likely to whet your appetite for the material, a process akin to turning over the soil and preparing it for seeding. You may want to use the same text for another period of spiritual reading, to allow a certain truth to sink in more deeply—especially to strengthen your recovery from rigid lifetraps that are resistant to change. When you find some material that is enriching and supportive of a healthy belief, stay with it until you begin to notice some weakening of your lifetrap.

As discussed in Chapter 3, keeping a journal is a useful tool in fostering self-awareness. At the end of a spiritual reading session, but not during it, you may want to ask yourself: How was the Holy Spirit touching me, moving me, challenging me, or consoling me during this time? Write freely and without censoring yourself—not to critically evaluate the text or to engage in intellectual speculation, but to record the graces of that period of reading in words. Your journal, then, can serve as a future source for spiritual reading, following the themes or lifetraps that are directly relevant to your emotional and spiritual well-being.

Finally, you may want to organize periods for shared spiritual reading with friends or prayer partners. If you are comfortable with groups, this may increase your motivation for practicing this discipline, even when you are personally experiencing a certain dryness that occasionally accompanies all spiritual practices. This gathering in faith is likely to support your lifetrap recovery, by enriching your appreciation for the texts and their witness to saving truths. Such groups are often available at most retreat centers and parishes.

# Epilogue

Overcoming lifetraps is a daunting challenge. These rigid and unhealthy beliefs and expectations that have their origin in childhood experiences of parents, siblings, and peers are reinforced by a lifetime of choices that more than likely support and defend their assumptions. If your lifetrap is *abandonment*, then you will likely choose partners and friends who are self-centered and rejecting, and your belief that intimacy and closeness are impossible dreams will be repeatedly reinforced. Or if your lifetrap is the belief that you must always focus on meeting the needs of others at the expense of your own needs, then you will likely attract those who make extraordinary demands on you without regard for your wishes or happiness. The effects of these lifetraps on your personal happiness and satisfaction are toxic. Lifetraps make it very difficult to feel satisfied with your life, and at least some degree of anxiety and depression are chronic companions. In addition, your relationships at work and at home are far less satisfying and productive than desirable.

This book has attempted to identify and describe various spiritual strategies and contexts for engaging in them, to supplement the enormous psychological contribution made by Jeffrey Young to the identification and treatment of lifetraps through Schema Therapy (ST). But even Young and Klosko acknowledge in their groundbreaking book, *Reinventing Your Life*, that change is not just the absence of lifetraps. They encourage readers "to look beyond the elimination of your individual lifetraps to an image of what will lead you finally to feel fulfilled, happy, and self-actualized."

Hopefully, this book has responded at least partially to this challenge for people of faith. The vision of a God Who calls each of us out of darkness into His own wonderful light, and

Who is committed to our growth in truth and holiness, is the basic motivation for engaging in the various psychological and spiritual techniques outlined in this book. The psycho-spiritual approach described in this book is designed not simply to help you to overcome lifetraps, by challenging those false beliefs and assumptions, but also to assist you in realizing more fully the truth of your being—a truth which can set you free to love yourself, others, and God, and in so doing to find the happiness that you so richly deserve.

# Glossary

## LIFETRAPS

**Abandonment**

The perception that significant others will not be stable or reliable sources of support and connection.

**Dependence**

The belief that one is unable to handle everyday responsibilities in a competent manner without considerable help from others.

**Emotional Deprivation**

The expectation that one's desire for a normal degree of emotional support will not be met by others.

**Entitlement**

The belief that one is superior to others and is not bound by the rules and regulations that govern others.

**Mistrust and Abuse**

The expectation that others will inevitably hurt, cheat, or manipulate me.

**Subjugation**

The belief that my needs, wishes, and feelings must be suppressed in order to meet the needs of others and to avoid criticism or retaliation.

**Unrelenting Standards**

The belief that one must strive to meet unrealistically high standards of performance, usually to avoid criticism.

## PRAYER FORMS

**Contemplatio**

To transform your ordinary experience by focusing on the many diverse ways that God is communicating Himself in the ordinary persons and events of your life.

**Lectio**

To inform yourself by the Word as it speaks to you about God and reveals your own authentic self.

**Meditatio**

To reform your mind to the mind of Christ, by applying your reasoning powers of imagination, memory, and understanding to your lived experience in order to see yourself and your life through a new lens.

**Oratio**

To ask for the grace to conform your will to God's plan for your life.

# References

Ainsworth, M.D.S. *Patterns of Attachment: A Psychological Study of the Strange Situation*. Hillsdale, N.J.: Erlbaum, 1978.

Barry, W.A., & Connolly, W.J. *The Practice of Spiritual Direction*. San Francisco: Harper & Row, 1982.

Bowlby, J. *A Secure Base: Parent-Child Attachment and Healthy Human Development*. New York: Basic Books, 1988.

Carrington, P. *The Book of Meditation*. Boston: Element Books. 1998.

Abraham H. Maslow's "unfinished theory." *Journal of Transpersonal Psychology*, 1995.

Enright, R.D. and North, J. (Eds.). *Exploring Forgiveness*. Madison: University of Wisconsin Press, 1988.

Fraiberg, S. *The Magic Years: Understanding and Handling the Problems of Early Childhood*. New York: Scribner, 1959.

Houdek, F. *Guided by the Spirit: A Jesuit Perspective on Spiritual Direction*. Chicago: Loyola Press, 1996.

Keating, T. *Intimacy with God*. New York: Crossroad, 1994.

Kohut, H. *The Restoration of the Self*. New York: International Universities Press, 1977.

Kornfield, J. *A Path with Heart*. New York: Bantam Books, 1993.

Linehan, M. *Cognitive Behavioral Treatment of Borderline Personality Disorder*. New York: Guilford Press, 1993.

Mahler, M.S. *The Psychological Birth of the Human Infant: Symbiosis and Individuation*. New York: Basic Books, 1975.

May, G. *Addiction and Grace*. San Francisco: HarperCollins, 1991.

Miller, W.R. (Ed). *Integrating Spirituality into Treatment: Resources for Practitioners.* Washington, D.C.: American Psychological Association, 1999.

Novello, J.R. *The Myth of More.* New York: Paulist Press, 2000.

Ornish, D. *Love and Survival: The Scientific Basis for the Healing Power of Intimacy.* New York: HarperCollins, 1998.

Pargament, K. I. *The Psychology of Religion and Coping.* New York: Guilford Press, 1997.

Pennebaker, J. W. *Opening Up: The Healing Power of Expressing Emotions.* New York: Guilford Press, 1997.

Roberts, K., & Cunningham, G. "Serenity: Concept analysis and measurement." *Educational Gerontology,* 1990.

Sanderson, C. & Linehan, M. "Acceptance and Forgiveness." In W.Miller (Ed), *Integrating Spirituality into Treatment: Resources for Practitioners* (pp. 199-216). Washington, D.C.: American Psychological Association, 1999.

Sperry, L. *Spirituality in Clinical Practice.* Philadelphia: Taylor & Francis, 2001.

Teilhard de Chardin, P. *The Divine Milieu: An Essay on the Interior Life.* New York: Harper, 1968.

Turkle, S. *Life on the Screen: Identity in the Age of the Internet.* New York: Simon and Schuster, 1995.

Wicks, R.J. *Touching the Holy.* Notre Dame, Indiana: Ave Maria Press, 1992.

Yalom, I. *The Theory and Practice of Group Psychotherapy.* New York: Basic Books, 1995.

Young, J.E. *Cognitive Therapy for Personality Disorders: A Schema-Focused Approach.* Sarasota, Florida: Professional Resource Press. 1990, 1999.

Young, J.E. & Klosko, J.S. *Reinventing Your Life.* New York: Dutton Publishers, 1993.

## Additional Titles Published by Resurrection Press, a Catholic Book Publishing Imprint

| | |
|---|---|
| A Rachel Rosary  *Larry Kupferman* | $4.50 |
| Blessings All Around  *Dolores Leckey* | $8.95 |
| Catholic Is Wonderful  *Mitch Finley* | $4.95 |
| Come, Celebrate Jesus!  *Francis X. Gaeta* | $4.95 |
| Days of Intense Emotion  *Keeler/Moses* | $12.95 |
| From Holy Hour to Happy Hour  *Francis X. Gaeta* | $7.95 |
| Grace Notes  *Lorraine Murray* | $9.95 |
| Healing through the Mass  *Robert DeGrandis, SSJ* | $9.95 |
| Our Grounds for Hope  *Fulton J. Sheen* | $7.95 |
| The Healing Rosary  *Mike D.* | $5.95 |
| Healing Your Grief  *Ruthann Williams, OP* | $7.95 |
| Heart Peace  *Adolfo Quezada* | $9.95 |
| Life, Love and Laughter  *Jim Vlaun* | $7.95 |
| The Joy of Being an Altar Server  *Joseph Champlin* | $5.95 |
| The Joy of Being a Catechist  *Gloria Durka* | $4.95 |
| The Joy of Being a Eucharistic Minister  *Mitch Finley* | $5.95 |
| The Joy of Being a Lector  *Mitch Finley* | $5.95 |
| The Joy of Marriage Preparation  *McDonough/Marinelli* | $5.95 |
| The Joy of Music Ministry  *J.M. Talbot* | $6.95 |
| The Joy of Preaching  *Rod Damico* | $6.95 |
| The Joy of Being an Usher  *Gretchen Hailer, RSHM* | $5.95 |
| The Joy of Worshiping Together  *Rod Damico* | $5.95 |
| Lights in the Darkness  *Ave Clark, O.P.* | $8.95 |
| Loving Yourself for God's Sake  *Adolfo Quezada* | $5.95 |
| Meditations for Survivors of Suicide  *Joni Woelfel* | $8.95 |
| Mother Teresa  *Eugene Palumbo, S.D.B.* | $5.95 |
| Personally Speaking  *Jim Lisante* | $8.95 |
| Practicing the Prayer of Presence  *Muto/van Kaam* | $8.95 |
| Prayers from a Seasoned Heart  *Joanne Decker* | $8.95 |
| Praying the Lord's Prayer with Mary  *Muto/vanKaam* | $8.95 |
| 5-Minute Miracles  *Linda Schubert* | $4.95 |
| Season of New Beginnings  *Mitch Finley* | $4.95 |
| Season of Promises  *Mitch Finley* | $4.95 |
| Soup Pot  *Ethel Pochocki* | $8.95 |
| St. Katharine Drexel  *Daniel McSheffery* | $12.95 |
| Stay with Us  *John Mullin, SJ* | $3.95 |
| Surprising Mary  *Mitch Finley* | $7.95 |
| Teaching as Eucharist  *Joanmarie Smith* | $5.95 |
| What He Did for Love  *Francis X. Gaeta* | $5.95 |
| Woman Soul  *Pat Duffy, OP* | $7.95 |
| You Are My Beloved  *Mitch Finley* | $10.95 |
| Your Sacred Story  *Robert Lauder* | $6.95 |

For a free catalog call 1-800-892-6657